PARAD
BY THE SLICE

Realize Your Dreams Through
Fractional Real Estate

JANET K. FISH

Accelerator Books

Editing by Terry Pfister.
Cover and interior text design by Eve Siegel.
Cover photograph of Janet K. Fish by Jarvis Photography.
Typesetting by Rainbow Graphics, Kingsport, TN.

ISBN: 978-0-9815245-4-2

Accelerator Books
P. O. Box 1241, Princeton, NJ 08542, USA
www.acceleratorbooks.com

9 8 7 6 5 4 3 2 1

In memory of my parents.
To my mother, whose love never wavered.
To my father—If I am only half the person you were,
I am content.

Contents

Foreword

When you hear about a rapidly growing industry in the $2+ billion range that caters very well to a hot market, including the 76 million baby boomers, take my advice: Don't hesitate . . . investigate!

Janet Fish's book, *Paradise by the Slice,* richly rewards you with the details and nuances of just such an industry.

I've known Janet Fish for years. She was at my "Loral's Big Table" number 9. It's a funny story because it wasn't until we worked out her financial baseline that she realized that she already had a half a million dollars in assets! At that time, she was working part time in a W2 job earning $250,000 per year. She was doing well, but she still had a deep yearning. She wanted freedom, independence, and security, and she wanted to pursue her passion for real estate, which included owning a luxury resort in Mexico. Janet took to real estate investing like she was born into it. Within a year, she quit her lucrative W2 job and raised enough OPM (other people's money) to swiftly become a heavy hitter in real estate investing.

Janet's laser-focused insights will assist you in making wise decisions when it comes to investing in this real estate niche. While reading this book, keep in mind that fractional real estate is the emerging winner of the vacation home market. When Janet talks about this topic, you should listen.

Janet will show you why fractional real estate is well

worth your consideration, whether you want to indulge in one or more luxury vacation homes for personal use or capitalize on the investment potential or both.

Janet's book delivers a solid strategy for finding and buying the best properties available while revealing the distinct advantages of fractional real estate ownership.

Fractional real estate ownership is not a timeshare. The differences are significant. You're not investing your wealth in mere chunks of time.

Fractional ownership is separate deeded ownership. It's yours to sell, rent, or leave to your heirs. Your piece of the property belongs to you in the form of a vastly more affordable share, one that you can enjoy for weeks or even months each year. Additionally, you can learn to leverage the extraordinary wealth-building opportunities it brings.

Fractional property development gives you yet another asset for your real estate portfolio. In response to rapidly escalating demand, real estate investors are developing these properties in dream destinations such as the Caribbean, Mexico, Central America, and New Zealand.

The concept is nothing new—Europeans have indulged in it for decades. What *is* new is the exploding popularity of this smart, advantageous ownership option across the United States and around the world. People now recognize that owning a second—or third or forth—home in such desirable locations doesn't have to mean breaking the bank or breaking your back doing repairs.

Paradise by the Slice is the definitive fractional real estate resource. Over the years, Janet has built a truly impressive real estate and fractional property portfolio using her keen eye and seasoned business savvy.

Whether fractional ownership is familiar to you, or you're new to the concept, this book is for anyone who has ever lounged on a serene ocean beach or gazed at snow-covered mountain peaks after the first powder of the season and thought, "I'd love to have my own place here." Today, like never before, that wish can become real, and the key is fractional real estate.

I'm a long-time advocate of building wealth with a diversified portfolio of investments, particularly in real estate. I highly recommend investigating fractional real estate through Janet's clearly written guidance in this book. She has a solid understanding, offers sound advice, and has a proven record of success. On a more personal side, Janet is a trusted friend whom I hold in high regard.

Janet's book offers detailed guidance and a wealth of wisdom. It will enlighten and excite you. Ready, go!

Loral Langemeier
Live Out Loud and
author of *The Millionaire Maker* book series

Acknowledgments

My special thanks to my friends for your enduring support, without judgment, when others thought I'd lost my mind. You *know* who you are.

To the Live Out Loud community, many of whom I consider my close friends. You have inspired me, believed in me, encouraged me, and given me the courage to achieve more than I ever thought possible. This book is dedicated to you.

To my sister Kathy for her never-ending confidence in me and for always being my biggest fan.

To Dave Brock and my sister Kathy for believing in my vision and backing that belief up by becoming investors.

To my brother Lew for challenging me and reminding me of the importance of family.

To Luna Moretti Fish for being exactly who she is, a lively, gentle spirit who always tells it like it is.

To Loral Langemeier for her fantastic mentorship, for providing a platform for me to grow beyond my wildest dreams, but more important, for her friendship.

To Will Mattox for being the catalyst I needed to create change in my life and for challenging me to step up and lead. Thanks also, Will, for your wise council, support, and partnership in our Mexico deal. I couldn't have done it without your guidance and belief in me.

To Tony Cordova for your vision, passion, and energy. You are one of a kind, and I am honored to be your partner.

To Coach Carl for showing me how to be a great coach by *being* a great coach.

To Debbie Miller, my best friend, for her enduring friendship, for being my sounding board and my rock as I jumped off cliffs that scared the you know what out of me. You are truly the nicest person I know.

To Dave Brady for being my friend and riding partner, always pushing me beyond what I thought I could do. You have a remarkable attitude toward life, and I have learned and continue to learn much from you.

To Laine Clifford, who taught me that a haircut is not a hair style and the meaning of friendship that withstands the test of time.

To Michael Ornelas for making my transition to life in South Lake Tahoe not only easy but great fun. Thanks for always supporting me and for introducing me into your inner circle. It means the world to me.

To Marian Woodard for walking with me, holding my hand on our journey toward spiritual awareness.

In memory of my dear friend and mentor, David O'Byrne, who taught me how to be a great salesperson and how to "walk gently amongst one another."

To Gemma Farrell for the opportunity to write this book. Without your help, I wouldn't have had the chance to realize my dream of sharing fractional ownership with countless others.

To Terry Pfister for your hard work and insights to make this book a reality.

To Elaine Gagne, someone who may even love Mexico more than I do, for always believing in me and giving me feedback when everything seemed new and somewhat overwhelming. Your partnership has been key to making Tequila Ranch and Cerritos Beach a reality. I look forward to being neighbors on the beach.

To Gary Bauer and Wendy Byford for showing me how to structure my businesses and my life and how to have fun doing it. You two are my inspiration.

To Ted Shuel for being my mentor, inspiring me to find my passion in land development, for coaching me through my partnership divorce, and for making me a better person.

To Heather O'Brien, Martha Hanlon, and Chris Williams, my high-powered women's mastermind group, for holding me accountable, making me uncomfortable, and pushing me to be even more than I thought I could be.

To Tana and Kaya for showing me unconditional love as only dogs can.

And finally, to Michael, my partner and my love, for showing me what is really important in life and for sharing his with me. "And we're still together."

CHAPTER 1

It's Time to Realize the Dream

Whether you're looking for a second home that will give you the ultimate satisfaction or considering real estate as an investment opportunity with a significant financial return, you too can realize your dream through fractional real estate.

Have you ever been on vacation and found yourself having one of those amazing "I could *live* here!" moments?

For me, the moment came while I was visiting Cabo San Lucas a few years ago. I was standing on an untouched beach, mesmerized by the deep blue swells of the Pacific Ocean stretching as far as my eyes could see. The sand was soft under my feet and the wind gentle in my hair. The weather was perfect—sunny, warm, and inviting—the sun high in the sky. I could hear the pounding of the waves on the sand and smell the saltiness in the air. The nearby city, with its small-town amiability and modern conveniences, offered a rich culture and a community full of smiling, congenial people. There was a special feel to that place. No doubt about it, I knew I was *home*.

It's something that most of us have experienced. You're on vacation in your favorite place in the world. Maybe you're on the beach like I was, or you're at the top of a mountain, ready to slalom through knee-deep powder. You look around you and think, "Could I actually own a second home here?"

You know you could invest in a timeshare, but you haven't heard many good things about those limited vacation home options. No, you want a place of your own, where your time and money will give you everything you're looking for—quality, luxury, value, flexibility, service, and access to the all the things you love to do. You'd like to think that you could buy a house or a condo, but the price tag in this kind of paradise puts the "heft" in hefty—and besides, you'd only be using the place for the chunks of time you have available. The rest of the time the place would sit empty.

I've been there on that beach and at the top of that ski run, and I've pondered those very same questions. That's how I came to learn about fractional real estate and how with a fractional property I could own my own *slice of paradise*—without a huge capital outlay, without the burdensome maintenance and typical headaches of homeownership, and with more services and amenities than I ever thought possible.

VISUALIZING YOUR VACATION HOME

When you dream about owning that second home, what do you imagine in your mind's eye? Perhaps for you it's mornings on the first tee, driving the ball in a long arc down the fairway toward the green. Later, you'll sip a cool drink with friends on your lanai. That's your idea of the good life. There's nothing like taking in the late afternoon sun as it sinks into the aquamarine sea.

Maybe you prefer to walk along a quiet, wooded path toward the lake, where you can fish or skip stones with the kids. How about a late breakfast on the veranda overlooking the water, where you can chat about the afternoon ahead? What do you feel like doing today? Do you want to play tennis? Peruse the local shops? Sit and read by the pool?

Or winter sports may be what you live for. Your dream is to walk right out your back door, step into your skis, and make your way to the lift. You've got the black runs on your agenda today. When you're done, the evening will include a quiet, romantic dinner in town.

If you too have dreamed of owning a second home in paradise, but the cost, the hassle, and the work involved with owning two homes have made you hesitate, this book is for you. You'd love to own your dream vacation home, and you want to know how. *Fractional ownership* is the answer you have been searching for.

You may have heard of fractional ownership before, but

you're not really sure what the term means. Perhaps it's all new to you, and you're keen to learn about it. Whether you are already retired and ready to buy a luxury vacation property or you are a successful businessperson looking for a get-away place for stolen weekends and that precious commodity called *vacation time*, fractional real estate has everything to offer you.

Fractional real estate, sometimes referred to as *shared ownership*, is deeded ownership of your dream vacation home at the right time, in the right place, and at the right price. With fractional ownership, you really can have it all! In Chapter 2 we'll get into the details of fractional real estate, but for now, let's slice it down to the key benefits. You want your very own slice of paradise, and this book will be your guide to how fractional real estate can make your dreams a reality.

IT'S YOUR SLICE

When you purchase a fractional property, you become the *deeded owner* of a sizable percentage of a luxury property. Fractional properties are high-end luxury homes or condos with shares typically ranging from 1/13 to 1/4. If you want to share ownership (and the cost) of a vacation property with your friends and family, you can. Several investors in my own Mexican properties are my close friends and family members.

The generous fractions really add up—each owner can

use his or her second home anywhere from four to twelve weeks a year. Unless you plan to live in your second home most of the year, it doesn't make financial sense to pour all your money into a solely owned property. Most people use their second home only at select times and during certain seasons, averaging three to four weeks per year. The rest of the time the house or condo remains locked up and unused. Unless you rent your property to other parties, your investment is just gathering dust (and interest payments). With fractional ownership, your property is ready when you arrive—secure, cared for, and maintained.

Inevitably I get asked, "Isn't fractional ownership like a timeshare?" Many people confuse fractional ownership with timeshare, and while they both are defined by ownership of "time" in a property, they are very different creatures. I'll cover these differences in greater detail in Chapter 3, but keep this in mind: Unlike most timeshares, you *own* your fractional property, and as the deeded owner, you benefit from greater flexibility and more time of use.

When it comes to other benefits, the level of service and amenities with a timeshare leave much to be desired. With fractional properties, you have ultra-high-end amenities and exceptionally high levels of service. You *own* your fractional property, and this means that you have all rights to it. You can rent it, sell it, and pass it on to your heirs. And you get to keep the appreciation.

Owned by Your Second Home

The concept of shared ownership, while compelling to most, may seem too risky for some people. Others just don't like the idea of sharing their home. If you're one of those folks who would rather opt for a solely owned property, be prepared to mix work with pleasure—and I do mean *work*. There's a good chance that the time you spend getting away from it all also will include such chores as home repairs, replacing home furnishings, housecleaning, and lawn care.

I don't know about you, but I don't get away from it all so that I can vacuum rugs, pull weeds, or clean out the gutters! That's like being owned by a second home. Owning a fractional property means leaving the work to someone else and freeing up your time for the activities you truly enjoy, such as painting watercolors outdoors, shopping for antiques, giving dinner parties, or just taking in the beauty of the nature around you. You can focus on the fun and let someone else handle the rest.

Sound expensive? With shared ownership, you will pay only a fraction (pun intended) of the maintenance costs versus the cost to maintain a full-ownership residence—and someone else does all the work!

IT'S YOUR IDEA OF PARADISE

Fractional ownership as an industry continues to grow year after year, and fractional properties now can be found in the most *desirable* locations in the world. We are talking about beachfront living in tropical destinations such as Mexico, Costa Rica, and the Caribbean and winter wonderlands in such world-class areas as Colorado, Canada, and Europe.

There are also luxury country club communities in Michigan and the Carolinas offering fractional ownership. You can retreat to quiet lakefront or hillside properties in Texas or Tuscany. If you'd rather spend some time walking to the urban beat of a city like New York or London, there are elegant fractionals just waiting for you. And for world travelers, shared-ownership properties are also available in Australia, Africa, and many other exotic locations. With fractional ownership, the sky is the limit—you can even own *multiple* slices all over the world.

In Chapter 3 we'll take a virtual tour of the most desirable vacation spots in the world and discover where the hottest fractional property investments are today. You can rely on the fact that there is a perfect fractional property just waiting for you and every other person dreaming about owning a slice of his or her own personal *paradise*.

It's Time for Lake Tahoe

Lake Tahoe is one of the world's most beautiful winter and summer playgrounds. I doubt that I am the only one who has come for a visit, found an ideal home away from home, and stayed for a lifetime. There is a spiritual feel to Lake Tahoe, and to really understand it, you have to experience it!

Winter here means weekend drives to skiing, snowboarding, and après-ski relaxation in front of a roaring fire in your living room. Summers beckon you to go boating or waterskiing, mountain biking, camping, or hiking through thick, lush forest full of birds and wildflowers. There are also all-season pleasures such as taking in the terrace view of the surrounding mountains and shopping the many one-of-a-kind boutiques. And, of course, there is the lake itself, certainly one of the wonders of the world.

The culture is small town meets high-end resort. Laid back and relaxed, everyone is friendly, whether you've lived here for years are visiting for the first time. Luxurious fractional properties are available in Lake Tahoe, and if this dreamy lakeside getaway has captured your imagination, go there and discover whether it's your idea of second home heaven.

IT'S YOUR PLEASURE

Luxury fractional properties come with a gourmet menu of services and amenities designed to enhance your vacation home experience. There are onsite spas, concierge services to fulfill your every request, cleaning services that won't let you lift a finger, and fine restaurants that cater to your dining pleasure. And you can have all this for a fraction of what you would pay with full ownership.

As the popularity of this type of ownership grows and more and more fractional properties become available, developers with extensive property portfolios now allow you to exchange your weeks with shareowners in other dream destinations. It's ski season for your property, and you're pining for deep sea fishing? Your management company can find you the perfect oceanfront property—and someone to bait the hook for you.

For most of us, vacation homes are all about the people we share our time with. As a true owner, you can decide to get away for some private time, bring the whole family with you, or just invite a couple of special friends. You also have the flexibility to rent your share when you have no plans to use it yourself. I know many owners who do just that to offset their investment or maintenance costs.

When it comes to your fellow shareholders, you can join with friends and family like I did or let the management company do the work for you. To that end, you also can get to know the other shareholders of your second home, or they can remain perfect strangers. When it comes to owning a fractional property, it's about flexibility, your pleasure, and peace of mind!

IT'S YOUR EQUITY

We all know that the most desirable locations in the world also tend to be the most expensive. Few people actually can afford to plunk down millions on a beautiful Caribbean beachfront house or a luxury townhouse in that ski Eden called Heavenly Valley.

Does this mean that you have to resign yourself to expensive rental properties or costly resort hotel packages? Not when shared ownership allows you to realize your dream while investing less money up front. You build equity in your home while you enjoy your very own deluxe accommodations in some of the most breathtakingly beautiful places on the planet.

Fractional real estate has *real* advantages, and its popularity as a solid, equity-building investment is booming. According to a 2008 national report on fractional properties,* close to $2.5 billion was spent on fractional properties as people diversified their investment portfolios by buying or building shared-ownership vacation homes and condominiums. With an estimated 79 million baby boomers retiring in the next fifteen years, demand for ownership of second homes is growing at a rapid rate. This is what makes

---

*2007 Annual Fractional Interest Report, Northcourse, *www.northcourse.com*.

fractional real estate such a smart, valuable, and beneficial opportunity for you.

IT'S ABOUT LIVING THE DREAM

In the next chapter we will dive into the details of fractional ownership, but first I'd like to share a little of my story because, chances are, you and I have a lot in common. I didn't start out as a land developer. In fact, I have come upon the career I love late in life.

Once upon a time, in a land far, far away, I was a successful corporate executive working for a major software company. Even back then I must have had real estate in my blood because I seemed to gravitate toward buying properties instead of luxury toys like my friends did. No cars and boats and clothes for me—I liked single-family homes, apartment buildings, and land!

My journey lead me to a dynamic investment community called *Live Out Loud (www.liveoutloud.com)*, where I forged strong connections with like-minded individuals who were interested in entrepreneurial endeavors that could build substantial wealth. Live Out Loud taught me about teamwork and leadership and has been instrumental in my involvement with fractional real estate.

By the time the corporation downsized my position, I had a strong portfolio of real estate and was looking to buy land and develop my own luxury resort. Many people have asked me, "How do you go from selling software to land development?" It only gets stranger to explain because the land I found and fell in love with was in Mexico! So now we're talking *international* land development.

Was I crazy to leave the comforts of corporate America and jump off the cliff? Well, maybe a little. Was I scared? Well, maybe a lot, but that didn't deter me because I was on a mission to find freedom from the rat race and to contribute, learn, and have more fun than I ever thought possible. One day I went from corporate mover and shaker to chief executive officer of my own real estate company, Breakaway Enterprises, LLC (*www.breakawayllc.com*). I chose that name for my company because it says everything about what motivated me to get into this industry.

Breakaway is a cycling term, meaning to take the lead by breaking away from the pack of riders (called the *peloton*). In cycling, team members take turns blocking the wind for each other so that the team leader can save his or her energy for the eventual move to the front position. In cycling, as in life as I see it, success depends on the *team*. With the support of my team, I broke away from the corporate norm and moved into an investment business that got my heart pumping. I can't help but relate to the cycling metaphor that inspired me to name my business, Breakaway Enterprises. I offer my clients the chance to break away from traditional, limited second home options into the life-enhancing world of shared ownership.

After personally experiencing the pleasure, fulfillment, and extraordinary wealth-building opportunities that come with fractionals, I felt compelled to write this book. I am fully confident that whether you're looking for a second home that will give you the ultimate satisfaction, or you are considering real estate as an investment opportunity with ample financial return, you too can realize your dream through fractional real estate.

IT'S TIME TO BREAK AWAY

In Chapter 2 I will walk you through the world of fractional real estate, followed by additional chapters highlighting some of the most alluring resort markets around the globe. These are the locations where fractional properties are already welcoming people like you. I'll also talk about the people you'll work with and how to choose a management company with your best interests—and the highest levels of service and satisfaction—in mind. Chapter 5 outlines the important and enjoyable "homework" behind selecting a property that's right for you. And Chapter 7 is designed for those of you who are interested in developing fractional real estate for its tremendous return on investment.

As you read this book, you will have questions, so feel free to contact me through my website at *www.paradisebythe slicethebook.com*. Helping you to discover your slice of paradise is my mission, and I'll be happy to help you find the answers.

So let this journey of discovery begin! It's time to break away from everything you've previously thought about how to own a second home.

CHAPTER 2

Fractional Ownership 101

Fractional ownership began in Europe, as people much like us asked themselves how they could maintain a primary residence in one town and own a second home in the heart of Paris or in a seaside haven along the Mediterranean coast. The key to their success was *shared ownership*. Today, this tried and true real estate opportunity is waiting for you throughout the United States and around the world. It's your turn to make your dream of second homeownership come true, and I am going to share with you how you can make it happen.

What is a *fractional ownership*? It's about enjoying your leisure time, be it in a private bungalow or dancing the night away in a cross-town bar. We know it's about reveling in a private refuge where you can walk out onto the veranda to take in the view of the Pacific Ocean or meander through a dense forest rolling across along the shoulders of the mountains. For you, it could mean relishing the landscape of the golf course or enjoying other favorite activities with your family. It's all about enjoying leisure time in a beautiful setting—and it's all *yours*.

Of course, you could enjoy these very same things by staying in a deluxe resort hotel or renting a summer villa, but you're interested in *owning* a second home. This is where fractional ownership comes through for you. With the purchase of a fractional property, you are the title owner of the second home of your dreams, with all the resort-location perks and none of the headaches that come with typical full ownership. You can use your share when it suits your schedule and lifestyle, rent to approved parties, keep it in the family, or sell it should you choose to do so.

This is true *ownership*, and your property—its costs, its amenities, and its equity—is shared among partners who are just like you. Your fellow shareowners are like-minded people who understand value, quality, community, and the benefits of only paying for what they use. To me, it just makes sense:

- Why buy the whole property if you will use only a portion of it?
- Why not own multiple properties rather than be a slave to just one vacation home?
- Why not own a share of a million-dollar home rather than be sole owner of more affordable property of less value?

In Terms of Fractional Ownership

When you look into fractional properties, you will see such terms as *private residence club (PRC), destination club, timeshare,* and *hotel condominium.* The industry defines fractional properties as properties having a square footage price of $1,000 or under. You are considered a private residence club owner if the cost per square foot exceeds $1,000. I believe that this is a somewhat arbitrary distinction because factors such as location and brand name influence price per square foot. For the purposes of this book, therefore, I use the terms *fractional ownership* and *fractional property* to include both traditional fractional interests and private residence clubs.

Fractional properties are usually located on prime real estate and feature a far superior level of service, amenities, and luxury. As a fractional property owner, you have a luxury second home free from the worry of upkeep, maintenance, do-it-yourself services, and other chores associated with full ownership.

The other types of properties—timeshares, destination clubs, and hotel condos—are not considered true fractional properties because you do not own a deed to the actual property, just the right to use it.

THE FACTS ABOUT FRACTIONAL OWNERSHIP

As you consider whether fractional ownership is for you, there are five key considerations to keep in mind:

- The *location* of your vacation home
- The *time* you actually will use your property
- The level of *service* you expect
- The *amenities* you want to enjoy
- The *value* you want to realize as owner of a second home

The *location* of your vacation home is more than a place you travel to—it is about what you experience when you're there. There's the relaxation and comfort you enjoy in each meticulously appointed room. It's the daily invitation to all the activities you enjoy, from soul-satisfying leisure time to pulse-pumping sports and recreation. Your fractional property must be a beautiful, inviting sanctuary for you and the people you love. Let's face it, a second home is where you will build years of meaningful memories.

The *time* you will spend at your second home is largely determined by your availability. Can you get away for weeks or even months? Are you like me, working in a business that you love and looking for weekend trips and smaller chunks of vacation time several times a year? Are you retired and want to spend a month in Mexico, a month in Tuscany, or travel to Aspen to ski once a month? You'll want to consider a fractional property where you have the freedom to schedule time away in a manner that fits your needs and your lifestyle.

When it comes to the *quality* of your experience as the deeded owner of your fractional property, it's all about the *service* you need for the lifestyle you desire. You want a property management company that will bend over backwards to make sure that you are satisfied. Their job is to ensure that everything runs as smooth as silk, from ensuring your golf clubs, fishing gear, or snowboards are ready to use to guaranteeing that your second home is always spotlessly clean and ready to welcome you.

Ah, the *amenities*! These benefits are what make shared ownership so appealing. Imagine such amenities as concierge service, twenty-four-hour maid service, a gourmet kitchen, prearranged food shopping, high-tech security, kids'/teens' clubs for the youngsters, a heated pool, and private, secure storage of your personal items so that packing and unpacking are unnecessary.

Finally, there's *value*. Your fractional property will be located in a world-class resort area, which in the past typically has meant shelling out the big bucks. Imagine spending a tenth of what you might have to pay for a solely owned home on the spectacular Mexican coastline or in a skiers' paradise like Colorado. Picture your equity and resale value growing year after year. You're not dreaming—fractional ownership offers just that.

FINDING THE RIGHT MARKET

Current trends tell us that second home seekers are property shopping in two types of resort destinations. The first is the mountain locations offering first-class skiing in winter and hiking, biking, and water sports in the summer. The second involves the sunny tropical oases where it's all about basking in the warm sun with an expansive ocean view. Fractional homeowners are also claiming their slice of paradise on lakeside properties where they can fish and boat to their heart's content and in urban hotspots where fine dining and going to the theater are an everyday delight.

If your preference is a vacation home in the mountains, where you can ski, hike through the alpine forest with family and friends, and indulge in fine dining and lively entertainment in the city when it suits you, it's all about glorious ski resort markets such as Lake Tahoe, Aspen, and Whistler, British Columbia. Fractional ownership in these locales offers you the ideal escape for weekend retreats or for multiple, shorter chunks of time throughout the year. I call these vacation home destinations the *driving markets* because fractional owners tend to pack up the car or SUV and drive there frequently throughout the year.

Pura Vida in Costa Rica

Pura Vida means "pure life," and it is no wonder that it is the official slogan of Costa Rica! Flanked by both the Atlantic Ocean and the Caribbean Sea on the East, the interior of Costa Rica features mountain ranges, volcanic peaks (with active volcanoes), and tropical rain forests teeming with wildlife. The eco-minded government carefully monitors development in Costa Rica. However, unlike other underdeveloped countries in this region, the land of *Pura Vida* offers you a rich selection of second home locations—including beachfront homes, gated hillside estates, and condos in the lively capital city of San Jose.

This Central American country has been a favorite destination of American and European travelers for years owing to its natural wonders, comfortable year-round climate, warm culture, and friendly people. It's no surprise, then, that fractional developments are springing up across this special country. If you want the good life—*Pura Vida*—Costa Rica offers a treasure trove of experiences.

If your tastes run more to a distant tropical paradise and your dream is about that idyllic oceanfront view, swimming laps in the pool, collecting seashells with loved ones, or playing golf or tennis every day, you're there. If, when you choose to get away, you plan to enjoy weeks or even full months of pleasure in your second home, for you, locations such as Cabo San Lucas, Costa Rica, and the Bahamas fit the bill, and because you will fly to your resort destination, these are what I call the *flying markets*.

Whether your heart's in the highlands of Canada or on the resort beaches of the Caribbean, once you know the type of location you prefer, it comes down to the all-important usage plan.

USING YOUR SLICE

Whether retired or still working, most of us live busy lives full of appointments and obligations. It's hard to get away as often as we'd like, and full ownership of a second home often can become more of a financial and maintenance burden (Care to mow the lawn?) than a source of leisurely living.

Fractional ownership is where you find a balance between the cost of ownership and the actual time you'll spend using your vacation property. The "balance" you find with a fractional property also can bring some surprising ownership benefits.

Tom is a high-level exec from Seattle who works for a San Francisco–based company, where several of his company's most important clients are also located. Tired of the impersonal hotel stays that come with his frequent trips to the Bay Area, and unwilling to pour money into renting an apartment, Tom decided to look into buying a condo. It wasn't long before he had to concede that the price tag was exorbitant, even for a tiny San Francisco studio. He also started to question whether a condo was the answer because full ownership meant furnishing the place, shopping for food, and doing laundry and time-consuming maintenance. Sure, he could hire a housekeeper, but it all started to feel like one big hassle.

Tom learned about fractionals from his real estate agent, and once he looked into several properties, it was clear that he'd found the right solution for his needs. His purchase of a deluxe fractional two-bedroom condo at 1/6 share, giving him eight weeks a year, fits in perfectly with his work schedule. Conveniently located downtown, the lavishly furnished property brought special shareowner benefits, such as food stocking, daily maid service, and an in-house chef for client dinners.

Tom *owns* his fractional condo in San Francisco, and therefore, he gets all the equity-building benefits of ownership. He is also able to expense most of his costs to the company as travel expenses. He has the absolute convenience of having a place of his own in the city (no more hotel rooms), and the cost is shared with his employer.

This is just one example of how fractional ownership has changed what it means to own a second home. As you'll recall, true fractional ownership shares range from 1/4 to a minimum of 1/13. When and how you use your property— the *usage plan*—are where all the slices come together to form the perfect pie.

The *driving markets,* such as Snowmass and Jackson Hole, draw people who are looking for easy access to their second home by car. Here, it's about the flexibility to schedule a weekend or one week per month so that you can ski in the winter and hike or mountain bike along the wildflower-covered mountain trails in summer. In this scenario, shared ownership at 1/4 share makes perfect sense. You get flexible access to your second home once a month, every month of the year, and you are paying a fraction of what it would cost as sole owner of a house or condominium. Most 1/4-share usage plans give an owner a specific week of each month, which then rotates. For example, in year one you have the first week of every month, in year two you have the second week of every month, and so on. This is referred to as a *rotating usage plan*, and it ensures that each owner gets Thanksgiving, the December holidays, the Fourth of July, and any other holiday every four years.

Luxury seaside destinations such as Guanacaste, Costa Rica, and Puerto Vallarta—the *flying markets*—attract fractional homeowners who would rather book their stay for weeks or even months. As a 1/12 shareowner, you are now able to enjoy your second home, say, for the whole month of March or April. Or you can use your share for two weeks, and rent out the other two weeks in your month. This is quite common with 1/12 ownership plans. It is also common for one buyer to purchase multiple months, either consecutively or spread throughout the year.

There are a variety of usage plans for both driving and flying markets. With *fixed* usage plans, you purchase a fixed time in a specific property and enjoy it year after year. Take note that certain times of the year are considered "premium," and you will pay more for them, such as the Fourth of July and the December holidays, Thanksgiving, and winter months in warmer climates.

Floating plans allow owners to choose the time they want to vacation each year, and *mixed* plans allow you to own a portion of your time as fixed and the balance as "space available." Finally, there are *hybrid* plans that combine fixed and floating plans as well as fixed plans that rotate each year. The key is to understand the usage plan of the property you are considering and to ensure that it fits in with the way you plan on using your vacation home or schedule. For more on usage plans, see Chapter 5.

When it comes to using your second home in a way that suits you and your schedule, fractional ownership does for the homeowner what no timeshare or solely owned property can do! You want family time at Thanksgiving in Breckenridge this year, but your scheduled time slot is for the week before the holiday? Because you work with a service-oriented management company, you can ask your management company to look into swapping time with the shareowner who owns the long weekend you want.

Slice Your Operating Costs

Your maintenance company will do everything possible to keep operating expenses to a minimum while keeping the luxury experience at a maximum. Monthly maintenance costs for your fractional property are shared among all the owners. While most general costs such as groundskeeping and pool maintenance are split equally, other costs are carefully tracked and paid by the shareowner who accrues them. The result: You enjoy lower year-round costs.

Some management companies are starting to recognize that different people desire different levels of service. These groups provide multiple level-of-service plans, such as a premium plan that might include an in-house chef or twice-daily maid service. If you wish to pay only for the services you use, chances are that there is a plan offering you à la carte services that fit your individual wants and desires.

Suppose that you know that it will be impossible to find the time to fly to your fractional property in Maui this coming October. Your management company can find suitable renters for your appointed timeslot. And *suitable* means screened, appropriate people who will respect your property—people you yourself would approve of if you were turning your primary home over to renters.

INVESTING IN PARADISE

You know the things that you value—your loved ones, your time, your pleasure, your future, and your peace of mind. Shared ownership adds that other item to the value list—your money.

In today's market, a solely owned condo in a premier

winter resort location such as Lake Tahoe or Aspen can cost from $1 million up to as much as $10 million. Townhouses and condominiums in sun, sand, and sea markets such as Puerto Vallarta or Hilton Head can cost from $1 million to $5 million. You adventuresome global travelers can expect to pay between $1.5 million and $15 million for an apartment in Paris or a villa in the Tuscan countryside. The realities are that fractional residences are *multi-million-dollar* properties that, without fractionalizing, might be out of your price range.

If you have piles of disposable income to spend and you're free as a bird to use a wholly owned property at your whim, then you probably put this book down pages ago. Or if you are someone who'd rather own a vacation home outright and you have the financial wherewithal and time to manage the upkeep, congratulations! There is nothing like the gifts of time and money for enjoying a luxurious second home.

The financial benefits and rewards of owning a second home require a solution that balances the money I have to spend with the time I have to use my vacation property. This is why fractional properties appeal so much to me. I invest less money and reap 100 percent pleasure and prosperity. I have my own slice of paradise (I should say *slices*)— that I own and build equity on—and I can say good-bye to the burden of babying my property. My second home pampers *me*. This is what I call real return on investment.

When More Is Better

If you prefer some variety, and your dream is to enjoy varied locales around the country or around the world, picture flying each February to your second home in Key Largo, where you can lounge, bodysurf, play tennis, and feast on your deck while the sunset paints the sky. Then it's July, and you drive to your *third* home in San Francisco to visit the extraordinary museums and dine at the finest Chinese restaurants outside China.

Or it's May, and you leave your Champs Elysees apartment for a café au lait before strolling over to the Louvre. Flash forward, and it's December, and you've left your mountainside condo to take a holiday sleigh ride with your sweetheart.

Imagine being able to tell your friends about your vacation *homes*—the one on Marco Island, the one in Sun Valley, and the one nestled in California's beautiful wine country. Or better yet, imagine inviting them to come along! I am not talking about little cabins or tiny apartments either. These are luxury, multi-million-dollar homes that will make you the envy of your friends and family.

Let's say that you are someone who loves the mountains, and your dream is to own a second home in or near Lake Tahoe. You know that full ownership of a luxury home will run you $1 million or more. Fractional ownership at 1/4 share, typically one week a month, will only cost about $300,000. You will pay one-quarter of the property taxes and maintenance fees, and your property will be ready when you are.

You like that seaside condo in Cabo San Lucas, with its sandy beaches and verdant golf courses surrounded by palm trees? Buy it outright, and you will pay well over $1 million for the three to four weeks a year you might use it. Buy a luxury resort fractional, and you could pay under $250,000 for a full month of sun worshipping and deep sea fishing—a month such as December or January when there's frigid weather back home.

It's clear that with shared ownership, the cost of owning a multi-million-dollar second home now becomes *possible*. Instead of plunking down $1.5 million on a home in one location, you can spend 10 to 30 percent of that amount and let your money work for you in other ways. You also have the option of buying multiple shares of the same property, which offers you even more time and flexibility to spend extended periods in your slice of paradise.

Let's talk about risk. An investment in a fractional property is about lifestyle and personal choice first and investment opportunity second. You will pay a premium for a fractional share, so your number one priority should be enjoyment of the property, not financial appreciation.

Having said that, resales of fractional shares historically have done as well as or better than those of timeshares or whole ownership. This could be explained by the the fact that resort locales rarely see depreciation, even in slow or declining markets. An investment in multiple fractional properties in diverse locations will tend to mitigate your risk. As one real estate market slows, another may see a growth in appreciation.

FRACTIONALS MEAN FULL SERVICE

If you're still on the fence about the benefits of fractional ownership over whole ownership, here's another example of what you also get if you choose to go the solely owned route: You've paid $1+ million for that Colorado ski chalet you've always wanted, and it's time to hit the slopes. You pull up to your property, but you can't get into the driveway because it's snowed in. While daydreaming about sitting in front of that roaring fire, you now spend your first hours shivering in the cold as you shovel foot after foot of that white stuff.

But wait—there's more! If you haven't already stopped at the local store on your way into town for food and wine, you'd better go out and pick up something for dinner tonight and breakfast tomorrow before you and your loved ones suit up to ski. Make sure that the water heater hasn't gone on the fritz and that the cable TV has been connected. Those dead bugs in the shower? The musty odor? Time to clean up and open the windows to air out the place—if they aren't frozen shut. Meanwhile, the slopes are calling. (Sigh.) You'll get there eventually.

Now imagine this: You pull right up to your fractional

home because the driveway has been completely cleared of snow. Someone is there to take in your bags, so don't worry about that. You and your excited guests race inside, where the rooms are clean and comfortable, and the fire is crackling in the fireplace. Your ski equipment is ready for you—all you have to do now is gear up. After hours on the runs, you return exhilarated and hungry, and you just open the fully stocked refrigerator or enjoy a delicious gourmet meal prepared by the management company's in-house chef—and all this for much less than you'd pay for full ownership.

This is fractional ownership! Unparalleled luxury, comfort, and service—the experience of having your every request fulfilled. Now it's time to start thinking more in-depth about where you see yourself as you immerse yourself in the beauty and comfort of your fractional home.

Is your dream second home in California? Mexico? On the other side of the world? Chapter 3 takes you on a virtual voyage around the country and around the globe, where shared-ownership opportunities abound and new deluxe fractional properties are being developed every day. Next stop: your slice of paradise!

CHAPTER 3

Choosing Your Slice

Wherever you envision your slice of paradise, you can find a major hospitality corporation or experienced smaller development company ready to hand you the keys to your state-of-the-art resort fractional residence. The urge to own a slice of paradise is rooted in human history, and for hundreds, if not thousands, of years, people have traveled to their favorite destinations to take pleasure in beautiful, spirit-feeding surroundings. This once used to be the bastion of the very wealthy, until the latter half of the twentieth century saw people—from the ultra-affluent to the hard-working middle class—buying summer homes and securing getaway properties for their leisure time.

Fractional homeownership in the United States originated in Colorado, as passionate ski buffs claimed the Rocky Mountain region as their slice of paradise. Today, fractional properties represent a new and innovative opportunity for anyone considering the purchase of a vacation home. Yet the mention of fractional real estate inevitably prompts the question, "Isn't fractional ownership just another way of saying you have a *timeshare?*"

Who can blame anyone for feeling a little skeptical? During the 1980s and 1990s, a significant number of people jumped on the timeshare bandwagon. While many timeshare owners have been satisfied with their choice, quite a few found it to be a bumpy ride.

The financial upside of timeshare development attracted major, reputable hotel chains. It also lured some less-than-honest operators who took the money and ran or who made provocative promises that were nearly impossible to fulfill. As too many timeshare owners have also discovered, resale prices for timeshares in today's market tend to be discounted, sometimes *heavily* discounted, and this has made timeshares far less appealing as an investment.

It's no wonder that I meet people every day who view anything that resembles a timeshare with trepidation. While both timeshares and fractional ownership are considered shared ownership, they are very different things. Fractional property is defined by deeded ownership, usage plans, and resale value. It's fair to say that not all timeshares deserve the bad rap. However, it is still essential to understand that fractional properties are *not* timeshares, and the differences between them are significant—beginning with the most important difference, you, the owner.

YOUR TIME, YOUR PLACE

Most likely you've worked hard for the money you have, and you're at the stage of life where you are ready to reap the rewards that your money has to offer. Since you're reading this book, this includes the idea of a vacation home in a location you love, where you can relax in the pleasure of ownership and enjoy all that a second home has to offer— when you want it and with all the amenities.

When it comes to a timeshare, the name says it all: You buy a share of *time*, but in most cases you do not hold title to the property itself. Most timeshares allow you to purchase what's called a *fixed-week interval*, and you get the right to use your timeshare for one week each year. Other timeshares are on a point system, where you purchase points and accumulate access to a week or more at one of multiple properties owned by a developer. Once you book your timeslot, provided your desired dates of stay are available, it's often difficult to make a change.

There is also the difference in the number of shareowners with timeshares versus fractional properties. A timeshare property, which is what I would consider a property with more than thirteen shareowners, typically has fifty-two timeshare "owners," which can severely limit the flexibility you want. Let's say that you decide that you'd like to get away for a week for some seaside R&R, but it's March, and your timeshare week is set for October. What do you think the chances are that you can exchange your week with the timeshare holder who owns the week you want? Grab your credit card, because you'll have far better luck with a nice hotel. And don't forget about the maintenance fees. Often upward of $1,000 per week, the cost of timeshare maintenance really can add up, making ongoing ownership not only costly but also disappointing in what you get for your money.

Fractional ownership gives you real security and real flexibility. Your 1/4 to 1/13 share means that you are one of only four to a maximum of thirteen shareowners, and you'll be sharing your dream second home with like-minded owners—a lot fewer of them! With fractional ownership, you also can reserve your preferred dates of stay more easily, and peak-season timeslots rotate equitably among the owners. Instead of battling for a holiday slot, you can count on spending one or more of the major holidays in your second home. It is also far easier to exchange your scheduled stay when or if your vacation plans change.

In my mind, a timeshare resembles spending a week on vacation at a nice resort, whereas fractional ownership means spending time whenever I can in a home I *own* and paying only for the time I use. The experience I have at my vacation home is richer, more relaxing, and more luxurious. I'm taken care of, and everyday responsibilities fall by the wayside.

Timeshares will remain a good option for buyers who best fit the timeshare owner profile: someone who is looking for the ability to book a traditional one- or two-week vacation every year. Millions of people enjoy just such an arrangement! But if you want your own slice of paradise, a bigger piece of a superior pie, then fractional ownership is for you.

FRACTIONAL PROPERTIES FROM THE BIG PLAYERS

I decided to become a developer of luxury shared-ownership resort vacation homes because I fit the profile of the fractional homeowner. I also knew that this kind of entrepreneurial endeavor would have some inherent risks. After doing some serious homework, I discovered something that dissolved away much of the "risk factor": The fractional real estate industry not only is growing in leaps and bounds year over year, but it also has received the enthusiastic endorsement of what you will recognize as the "big players" in the ultra-high-end hotel and resort industry.

You'll recognize these players as some of the name brands that are synonymous with five-star resort living—The Ritz-Carlton, Fairmont Hotels & Resorts, Four Seasons Private Residences, Hyatt Vacation Ownership, and Marriott Grand Residences. These and other renowned companies, some of which have been into timeshares, are now moving into fractional properties in a big way because of vacation homebuyers like you and me.

If you need confirmation that fractional ownership is an established method for owning your own slice of paradise, look no further than the renowned luxury resort hotel brands that are currently developing fractional properties all over the world. For example:

- Fairmont Hotels & Resorts has fractional properties ready for purchase or in development in such ideal sun-and-sand destinations as Anguilla, British West Indies, Acapulco, and Palm Desert, California. They are also offering desirable city fractionals in San Francisco, New York City, and Dubai.

- Four Seasons Private Residences offers exclusive private homes in such idyllic vacation spots as Jackson Hole, Wyoming, Florence, Italy, and the "Pearl of the Pacific," Bora Bora.

- Hyatt Vacation Ownership is selling deluxe fractional properties in Carmel, California, Key West, Florida, and Breckenridge, Colorado.

There are smaller independent development companies, such as The Timbers and the St. Regis Club, that offer luxury fractional cottages in Oregon, lakefront fishing havens along Lake Superior in Michigan, first-class condos in Toronto, wine country getaways in Napa or Tuscany, and beautiful beachfront condos in St. Thomas and Cabo San Lucas.

The bottom line: Wherever you envision your slice of paradise, you can find a major hospitality corporation or an experienced smaller development company ready to hand you the keys to your state-of-the-art resort fractional residence.

After my first few trips to Cabo San Lucas, just getting off the plane had me immediately feeling the magic that is Mexico. Laid back and relaxed, the air itself calmed me. I yearned for an extended escape and knew I was not alone. This is why I selected Cabo San Lucas for my fractional property development. My own preference for this area was my first indication that there are literally thousands of people just like me—busy, successful professionals—who are seeking those rejuvenating escapes to a second home.

You'll hear more about my story and my experience as a fractional property developer in Chapter 7. For now, let's turn our focus on the fun part of owning a luxury vacation home—your idea of *paradise* and where your slice is waiting for you.

Defining the Destination Club

Destination clubs are the fastest growing segment of the luxury resort ownership industry. They are typically nonequity membership clubs where you pay an initial and substantial membership fee, in addition to annual dues, in exchange for a sizable chunk of time in some of the finest high-end resorts in the world. A destination club often will give you access to a vast network of exclusive multi-million-dollar vacation properties around the world, which has made these clubs popular with wealthy folks who have formerly owned and maintained multiple homes.

The advantage: If you yearn for a different vacation experience each year, traveling to the far corners of the world and always traveling to a different locale, destination clubs afford you the opportunity to do just that. While very expensive to join, destination clubs offer a vast array of locations to bask in the lap of luxury.

The disadvantage: A destination club is a non-equity club, meaning that you have the right to access properties owned by the club for a specific number of days per year, but you have no ownership rights to the underlying real estate. You don't hold title to any of the properties, and as such, you do not share in any of the appreciation.

Simply put, destination clubs offer vacation ownership, whereas fractionals offer true *home*ownership.

SURF, SNOW, AND CITY LIGHTS

Unless you are buying a second home for business or investment purposes, you will choose a slice for your personal use—a slice that stirs your appetite for pleasure and personal satisfaction and fits your lifestyle. It will be the retreat where you savor time with family or friends as you head off to ski, splash in the pool, sail, scout for whales or scarlet macaws, or wander the colorful art gallery scene.

While some of us crave the sea and sand, others of us long for moguls and cozying up by the fire. You may enjoy the elegant sophistication of the "City of Light," whereas I may prefer nibbling on fresh crab on Pier 39. No matter what you claim as your idea of paradise, fractional ownership is the key to living the dream. Fractional properties in today's market are exploding in popularity, and there are lavish fractional residences sprouting up in some very exotic areas around the world.

Let's look at the four areas where this $2 billion industry is well established and growing in leaps and bounds: the United States, Mexico, Canada, and the Caribbean.

Your Slice of the United States

The United States leads the way when it comes to fractional homeownership opportunities, according to the most recent industry information.* A whopping 54 percent of all fractional properties purchased are found in the United States, with Colorado and California having the lion's share of available fractional homes. When you look at *why* people are buying their resort fractional vacation homes in these locations, the *where* makes perfect sense.

Colorado, birthplace of fractional homeownership in the United States, is home to dozens of fractional developments in world-famous ski resort towns like Aspen, Vail, and Beaver Creek. The people who love the rush of winter sports are also lured here by the year-round beauty of the mountains, forests, lakes, and wildlife. In addition, for those

---

*The 2008 Northcourse survey, *www.northcourse.com*.

times when you're ready to paint the town red, there's easy access to trendy retail shops, excellent restaurants, and delightful evening entertainment.

Moving west, the state of California is a uniquely exceptional pie when it comes to choosing your slice! For the beachcomber, there's the sun-washed beauty of San Diego and Santa Barbara. For cosmopolitan flavor and stirring, romantic views of the Golden Gate Bridge—and some of the world's most exceptional restaurants and unforgettable rides on the cable cars—there's San Francisco. If you want skiing, snowboarding, mountain biking, kayaking, hiking, and a relaxed, carefree spirit, Lake Tahoe is second to none.

Looking at the United States as a whole, you'll discover that fractional properties are developing rapidly from coast to coast, as well as in many of the most exclusive resort vacation areas you can think of. Popular destinations such as sunny, sultry Florida now feature fractional second homes in desirable hot spots like South Beach, Jupiter, and Naples.

If you are looking for golfing at some of the top courses on the circuit, as well as serene living along the shore, check out Hilton Head in historic South Carolina. Buyers of second homes drawn to the desert can find captivating resort fractionals in Las Vegas and Scottsdale—Arizona's golfing Mecca.

Vermont is not only a renowned winter wonderland for skiing during the colder months, but it is also a year-round destination for fractional homeowners who want to take in the beauty of nature, celebrate maple season each spring, and take each day at an easier pace. Heartland states such as Michigan, Minnesota, and Missouri offer deluxe fractional lodges where the fishing is great, the accommodations are spectacular, and the service is superb.

There is little doubt about the growing popularity of fractional properties in the United States. In fact, you can find the second home you've always wanted in thirty-eight of the fifty U.S. states—and each year the number of available fractional properties continues to rise.

Bienvenidos to Mexico

As we move south of the border, it's easy to see how Mexico could hold immense appeal for fractional homeowners. Framing the Baja Peninsula are miles of dreamy beaches and colorful towns such as Todas Santos, La Paz, and Cabo San Lucas, where the surrounding waters beckon the experienced deep sea fisherman and the novice snorkeler.

Acapulco has enchanted vacation homeowners for decades with its gorgeous high-rise condos along the legendary semicircular bay. There's an amazing array of water sports available, such as jet skiing, power boating, and parasailing. Ixtapa fractionals also feature first-class oceanfront accommodations, where you can scuba dive, fish, or just spend long, leisurely hours lying in the sun.

Imagine spending your leisure time in timeless Cancun, where you can explore centuries-old Mayan ruins in the morning, horseback ride on the beach in the afternoon, and dance the night away under the stars. There are fractional homes available in lush Mexican coastal towns that are just a few hours' driving distance from most locations in the American Southwest.

Mexico is a welcoming neighbor to the south, and retirees and vacation homeowners are enthusiastically accepting the warm, friendly invitation. We'll explore more about Mexico in Chapter 6. You also can discover more about fractional ownership in Mexico by visiting *www.paradisebytheslicethebook.com*.

Leisure Living in Canada

Our neighbor to the north is also welcoming fractional owners with open arms. With properties ranging from upscale urban condos to luxury lakeside cottages, Canada has quickly become one of the most desirable locations for prosperous retirement living and high-end vacation homes.

If your tastes run to haute cuisine and high fashion, you'll find your stylish fractional residence in Toronto, Canada's cultural, entertainment, and financial capital. Looking for more tranquil living? Just a couple hours outside this wonderful city are fractional single-family homes along woodland lakes—perfect for fishing, boating, or dining al fresco on your deck.

For historical flavor and the élan of old Europe, Montreal offers fractional properties in the many special neighborhoods for which this city is known. You can find your second home near the cobbled streets and centuries-old buildings of the Old City. Or your second home may be near the dazzling nightlife along renowned Sainte-Catherine Street, where you can find everything from quaint sidewalk cafés to the liveliest nightclubs and cabarets this side of Paris.

The shining star on Canada's Pacific coast is Vancouver, an amazingly diverse city that offers the fractional home-owner a veritable feast of things to do. The people-friendly climate and nature-rich environment provide tantalizing year-round activities from golfing twelve months a year to skiing on Whistler Mountain or hiking in the peaceful "Pacific rain forest."

The Canadian Rockies are surely one of those most ma-jestic mountain ranges in North America, and this is where you will find Banff. Fractional living here opens your world to towering peaks, pastoral fields of wildflowers, and awe-inspiring waterfalls! You can ski, play golf, take nature hikes, and stroll through the many wonderful boutiques and galleries. Fractional ownership in Banff may be ideal for the nature lover who also wants to enjoy the best a city has to offer.

The Caribbean for Fun in the Sun

The Virgin Islands, Bermuda, Jamaica, Grand Cayman—I am willing to bet many of us, at one time or another, have run to these spectacular oases and let the lazy island vibes ease away the stress. Featuring miles of white sandy beaches and the sparkling turquoise sea, St. Thomas, St. John, and St. Croix offer the fractional homeowner an intimate beachfront home or a hillside villa with the finest accommodations and five-star amenities. St. Bart's takes that island flair and adds a splash of Franco flavor to its offerings. Here, you'll find superb restaurants where the cuisine is all French and the ambiance is all "island." Limited development here is designed to ensure that this island treasure stays as quaint as its fractional properties are opulent.

Fractional living in the Cayman Islands provides a variety of personal pleasures in a rich, gentle island culture. After parasailing on the Seven Mile Beach with the kids, you can enjoy Caribbean lobster served under the palm trees. Maybe you'll windsurf later in the afternoon or take the pirate cruise. It's up to you because it's your slice of paradise!

Fractional ownership in the Caribbean Islands takes the pleasures of sand, sun, and sea to a new level, where luxury and island leisure combine to create a feast for the fractional homeowner.

Buying in Bermuda

Bermuda boasts an enviable climate and a beautiful location—just a quick flight from the East Coast of the United States—and sophisticated travelers have long dreamed of owning their slice of paradise here. In the past, only the very wealthy have been able afford to buy a vacation home in Bermuda owing to stringent government restrictions on real estate sold to foreigners.

Today, fractional ownership makes the dream of vacation homeownership more accessible because Bermuda resort fractionals are categorized as "tourism properties." Instead of paying millions of dollars for the rare, solely owned vacation home that is available for purchase, you can now pay a fraction of the cost and still enjoy deeded ownership on this exclusive Caribbean island.

FINDING FRACTIONALS IN FARAWAY PLACES

Fractional real estate started in Europe, so it's no surprise that shared-ownership properties abound across the Continent. However, the newest frontier of fractional real estate is in international flying markets that many people may find surprising. If you're the type who would like to explore second home possibilities in faraway countries, you'll be pleased to hear that fractional homeownership is becoming more appealing and affordable in such places as Central America, South Africa, and New Zealand.

Costa Rica is already a haven for American and European retirees who want vacation homes. There are sumptuous private fractional residences tucked away in the lush rain forests and in the mountainous regions where coffee plantations blanket the hillsides. Of course, the country's beautiful coastlines provide perfect locations for glamorous oceanfront living.

South of Costa Rica is Panama, and this secret paradise is among the newest hotspots for fractional homes. There are stylish, well-appointed beachfront estates available, and they are managed by companies dedicated to quality and service. Panama, including its sophisticated capital of Panama City, ranks high in resident and tourist safety, which means that you can enjoy the nightlife there after taking guided tours into the undeveloped wilderness of the rain forest.

Shared ownership in South Africa is also booming, and that's because shareowners can purchase luxury fractional waterfront villas and hillside estates with access to great golf courses and wild animal preserves at affordable prices! Beachfront properties in New Zealand are also being developed, and fractional homeowners are finding that leisure living near New Zealand's Bay of Plenty offers plenty of reasons to purchase a shared-ownership property.

This list is really an "appetizer course" for you because new deluxe resort fractionals are being developed in exotic locations every day. Wherever people like you or I imagine owning a second home, fractional ownership is opening the door. This is why the time is now to take a definitive step toward owning your own slice of paradise.

Whether you are interested in shared ownership in a foreign country or one closer to home, you'll want to start by doing your homework. Successful ownership of your fractional slice starts with *due diligence*. Begin by checking out available properties online, and use the questions in Chapter 5 as a starting point for your research.

Remember: Different countries will have different restrictions to property ownership, and you'll want to make sure that you cross your T's and dot your I's before you sign on the dotted line.

CHAPTER 4

Your Life in Paradise

Fractional ownership is about a luxurious lifestyle in an enviably upscale environment. And when it comes to service, it's all about you.

Lake Tahoe is one of those special places that had me at "Hello." As a satisfied resident of the San Francisco Bay Area, I was looking for a weekend destination where I could ski in the winter, ride my bike in the summer, hike majestic peaks around fields of wild flowers, and escape from the hustle and bustle of my successful business. Lake Tahoe captivated me with its close proximity (about a three-hour drive from San Francisco); the natural splendor of the lake and the mountains; the exceptional skiing, hiking, and biking; and the compelling mixture of upscale resort living in a charming small-town culture. Being there made me feel like I was galaxies away from my busy life. It quickly became one of my favorite homes away from home.

You know the feeling. Second homeownership is more about what you savor and experience when you're there than simply having a street address. Yes, location matters, and by now, you may have an excellent idea of just where your second home will be. You are also keenly aware of the activities that fill your spirit with joy and peace.

The experience of fractional ownership, including the pastimes that delight you most, has as much to do with the daily *lifestyle* as the location. While the location is key, it's the amenities that put it over the top. This is why this chapter presents a sampling of the marvelous amenities and services available at today's fractional developments. As you read, consider your personal lifestyle needs—present and future—and connect them to the experiences you want to have in your fractional vacation home. This is a winning formula for finding your true slice of paradise.

A DAY IN PARADISE

Fractional homeowners often compare daily life in their second home with an extended stay at a four-star resort hotel—except that the property is *theirs*. Picture this scenario: A limousine meets you at the airport and collects the luggage you'll never have to carry again. There are no bulky skis, golf bags, or fishing gear to lug because they are already waiting for you at your resort fractional.

When you arrive at your vacation home, you are greeted by a friendly face at the front desk, someone who knows you, has anticipated your arrival, and understands your every need. You walk into your posh private residence, where the air is fresh and the temperature is perfect. The rooms are spotless and elegantly furnished. After turning on the new top-of-the-line stereo system, you gaze out at the expansive view through your huge picture window. You can unpack your luggage, or it can be unpacked for you—it's your choice.

You're ready to relax into vacation home living, and this means having a glass of wine. No worries. Your wine rack is fully stocked, and your favorite cheese is in the latest-model refrigerator. When you're ready to ease the tension out of your muscles, climb into the Jacuzzi. To learn about the latest happenings in town, you can call the twenty-four-hour concierge. He'll know how to procure those impossible-to-get tickets and reservations at your favorite restaurant. Before you go out, leave the dishes—the maid will clean up and turn down the beds for you.

AT YOUR SERVICE

The quality of your experience is in the hands of a very important entity—the management company that oversees and/or operates your property. This group of resort living professionals is responsible for selecting the first-class furnishings and legendary services you can expect every time you arrive. They are also in charge of the amenities—those captivating extras that enrich your leisure time—and as you'll see, the list can be extensive.

One of the primary services offered by your management company is overseeing the yearly calendar and working with you to ensure that you can rest easy about your travel plans. The managers also will assist you with renting out your unit if the rental option is part of your property's rules and regulations.

If you choose to sell your fractional share, the management company also can aid you in the resale process. You'll discover that some developments insist on first right of refusal if you decide to sell so that other shareholders have the option of adding an additional share to their portfolio. This actually can make your resale more cost-effective and convenient.

Aloha to Fractional Living

Hawaii is one of the most in-demand American resort markets, and it is easy to understand why. Fractional properties in the Hawaiian Islands offer that blend of high-style and laid-back island life that makes you feel like you're in your own private Eden. Enchanting Waikiki fractionals can be found close to those famous golden-sand beaches and minutes away from exciting shopping, dining, and entertainment venues. You'll also find serene ocean-view villas on Kauai, where the first tee is just a short stroll away.

The most convenient way to peruse Hawaiian fractionals is to go online first. Then treat yourself to a trip around the islands to see the fractional com-

munities firsthand. Most reputable real estate companies can advise you as to what is available, and
Chapter 5 will provide you with a detailed checklist
of questions to ask.

Living Areas for the Good Life

Sole ownership of a second home usually means inheriting
the physical condition of the home and the decor style preferred by the previous owners. This includes the foundation
and the twenty-year-old furnace, as well as the path-worn
carpeting and used kitchen appliances. You might find yourself having to cope with baby blue walls or floral wallpaper
trim while you use precious vacation time updating the
decor and appliances.

Because you'll need furniture, factor in some more time
to shop for chairs, lamps, and bedroom sets. Plan to plop
down more money on an entertainment system and decora-
tive items. You'll also need to arrange for phone, cable, and
heating and air-conditioning services. And unless you're
into out-of-the-box finger food, don't forget about shopping
for cookware, dinnerware, and groceries.

Some adventuresome people will read this and say,
"Sounds like fun!" I am *not* one of them. To me, a second
home is about total comfort amid beautiful, sumptuous surroundings. With a fractional vacation home, this is exactly
what you get. Your fractional home, be it a two-bedroom
townhouse or a five-bedroom villa, will come fully furnished

and carefully appointed in a way that meets or exceeds the standards at most exclusive resort hotels.

You can expect exquisite high-end furnishings presented in a subtle, natural-color palette. There's a flat-screen high-definition television and stereo system with surround sound ready for you, as well as high-speed Internet service. Master bedrooms are masterfully styled, offering king-size beds with quality linens and spreads, fine furniture, and a peaceful ambience.

Kitchens are spacious and include new stainless steel appliances, granite or stone countertops, and roomy cabinets stacked with select cookware, dishware, and serving utensils for special dinner parties. Most fractional properties include one and a half private baths or more, along with a private whirlpool and sauna, and they are always appointed with towels and your favorite toiletries. There's even a roomy den or private office, which can be converted easily to an additional guestroom.

Living in Style

Many fractional developments feature an interior decor style that visually reflects the local flavor you love—such as glamorous island living in the Caribbean, urban savoir faire in San Francisco, and alpine chalet chic in Colorado. No matter what the individual style, your fractional home will offer a cordial luxurious atmosphere sure to delight you and your guests.

Many fractional development websites enable you to take a virtual tour through their units. Check out how they have designed and furnished each room, and see if the property fits your practical and pleasure-related needs.

At Your Service

A savvy management company will be dedicated 24/7 to offering you premier service. While many services are included in your monthly assessment, some services may be provided à la carte, such as discounted tickets, twice-daily maid service, or in-house chef services. The extra fees will vary, but be aware that certain fractionals may charge a higher rate for by-request services based on the type of service offered, the intrinsic value of renowned brand names, or the operating expenses that come with more exclusive locations.

Here are some of the services that are typically offered with fractional ownership:

Before You Arrive

- House cleaning and maid services
- Temperature control
- Snow removal in winter
- Prearrival shopping and stocking of foods, beverages, toiletries, and other necessities

- Transportation service from the airport
- Removal of your personal items from safe, secure storage and readying them for your use
- Prearrangements for yachts, fishing charters, rental vehicles, bicycles, tee times, dinner reservations, etc.

When You Arrive

- Valet parking of your vehicle if you choose to drive to your vacation home
- Bellman services for your luggage
- Quick, convenient check-in
- Arranging of tours, special excursions, tee times, and more

While You Are There

- Twenty-four-hour concierge service for finding local information, making dinner reservations, and taking care of any special needs
- Daily maid service for cleaning and changing linens so that you can focus on fun
- Restocking the refrigerator
- Ski and/or golf valet services
- Hunting and fishing guides
- Discounted greens fees and priority tee times
- Discounted lift tickets

When You Leave

- Lock-off areas for in-unit storage of personal items
- Fast, easy check-out
- Transportation to the airport or retrieval of your clean, freshly detailed car
- Return of skis, clubs, bikes, binoculars, etc. to storage
- Verification of your next trip to paradise

More and more management companies are contracting with exchange companies, giving you the option of using your fractional share at the townhouse or villa you purchased or enjoying your leisure time at one of their other properties. For people who want some variety in their location or the activities they enjoy, this is a service custom-tailored for you.

Savor the Day Spa Experience

Fractional ownership offers real perks when it comes to personal care, allowing you to look forward to enjoying the onsite whirlpool or the full-service day spa. Besides relaxing massage therapy, manicures, and pedicures, your property's day spa may also provide yoga classes and healing treatments for your mind, body, and spirit. There are even shared-ownership properties that offer long, leisurely soaks in private hot springs.

If there is a premier day spa in close proximity to your property, your development may opt to offer you preferred membership there—whatever best serves the needs and desires of the shareowner.

Amenities Galore

Because such words as *private, exclusive, luxurious,* and *deluxe* define the experience of fractional homeownership, the onsite amenities will remind you every day that you're living in paradise. Waterfront retreats often will give you direct access to a private beach, frequently for the sole use of the development's shareowners. There's usually a beach house as well for towels, snacks, and beverages.

Fractional resort ski area properties may have special ski-in, ski-out units. All you do is walk out your back door— where the staff has your gear waiting for you—and step into your skiis, push off, and you're on the slope on your way to the lift.

Many developments also tailor their amenities to couples with children. A special kids' clubhouse may be on the premises, and younger residents can take junior classes in skiing, golf, sailing, or fly fishing. When it comes to fractional living, even the youngest residents are pampered.

As a shareowner, exclusive amenities such as private swimming pools, exercise and fitness facilities, tennis courts, and access to some of the best golf courses in the area also are part of your experience. Whatever activities you enjoy, there is a fractional property that provides them. This is your life in paradise!

FINDING THE RIGHT FRACTIONAL PROPERTY

Let's take a look at Don and Lisa, a couple living in Silicon Valley with their two preteen children. Don works long hours for a high-tech firm, and he treasures his leisure time with his wife and kids. They are an active family, and the ski-fanatic parents taught their children to ski at a young age. Besides negotiating moguls, they also enjoy biking, hiking, camping, and water sports of every variety.

This is a family that has regularly escaped on weekends to Lake Tahoe, and they have always dreamed of owning a house there. The high real estate prices have made that option beyond their reach. They have even entertained the idea of buying a house there with friends and family, but they could never seem to pull it off.

When Don and Lisa looked into fractional ownership, they saw the fit immediately. They knew they would use the property for long weekends and a couple of full weeks during the year. The development agent assured them that their shared-ownership contract allowed them to lend the home to friends, or they could rent it out. Don got turned on by the fact that he could lend his fractional property to business associates as a business perk. And instead of paying $1+ million for a home, they paid just over $300,000, becoming deeded, equity-building shareowners.

The fractional development they chose offers Don, Lisa, and their children the ski-in, ski-out privileges they didn't think they could afford. There are also three luxuriously appointed bedrooms, a private sauna, and plenty of room for Lisa to relax and read while her kids play video games on the wide-screen TV.

The private storage means the days of lugging skiis, kayaks, and bikes back and forth from Palo Alto to Lake Tahoe are over. Summertime means hiking and water sports, and ownership at this development gives the kids access to sailing and scuba lessons, as well as a teen club. The family's favorite ritual? The first night always includes a special dinner prepared by the development's onsite chef.

How's that for your life in paradise? Fractional ownership is undeniably appealing to people looking for a second home because it means living in your favorite place and enjoying superior amenities and an extraordinary level of service. Of course, all this sounds provocative—but how do you know if a fractional property is right for you? How do you know if a shared-ownership property offers you the lifestyle, service, and amenities that you desire? It's time to determine if the development you've discovered is *your* slice of paradise.

Doing Your Due Diligence

Being in the know before you buy means that you can better discern whether a select fractional property is a slice of paradise that will truly offer you years of satisfaction and pleasure. You've decided that it's time to purchase the second home of your dreams, and your mind is set on a deluxe resort fractional in Vail, the Virgin Islands, or on the Baja Peninsula. Since you're reading this book, I assume that you are a knowledgeable consumer who knows that getting all the facts is imperative to making an informed decision. This chapter is about doing your due diligence, and in it I'll outline essential questions to ask along your journey toward purchasing your dream home.

Buying a vacation home can be an emotional decision, especially if you are in love with a certain location. Remember that an informed choice is one that gives you lasting peace of mind, free from worries or regrets—and that will add immeasurably to the serenity of lounging on your private beach in Cozumel or wherever you call *home*. There will be no second-guessing or buyer's remorse if you do your homework upfront.

Due diligence starts with *you*. Before you sign any paper-work or make any final decisions, ask yourself these important questions:

- Is this a fractional property that I *want* to own?
- If I could manage it financially or had all the time in the world to spend here, would I buy it as full owner-ship?
- Does the usage plan fit my lifestyle and the amount of time I have available to use the property?
- Does this property feel special? Does it make me feel like I'm staying at just another resort, or do I feel like I am *home?*
- Does the property reflect my taste and lifestyle?
- Will the property meet my future needs?

If you can answer "Yes" to these questions, you are on your way to finding your slice of paradise. The first step is to determine if a certain development fits your needs and wants. The next step is to ask, ask, and ask questions!

So, you've narrowed down your list of potential second home sites, you've gone online and done your homework, and you feel excited about taking the next step. Here are some guidelines to help you make that final decision:

Go there. There is no substitute for being there! Few of us would buy a primary residence based solely on attractive digital images and clever website copy. Go see what the property physically looks like and how well it is maintained. Check out the quality of the accommodations, the pool, the clubhouse, the storage facility, and transportation into town. Become familiar with every service offered. Get to know the management company staff. And while you are there, be sure to talk to existing fractional homeowners about their experiences living there.

If you plan to purchase a fractional property abroad or are unfamiliar with a region, plan to spend some time there—get to know the locals, and get a feel for the culture and the community. This is your second *home*, and you want to make sure that your decision is one you will enjoy for years to come.

Get it in writing. Insist on written documentation, and then take the time to read every document thoroughly. Ask any and every question you have, and if a certain provision is unclear, keep asking questions until you get a clear explanation.

Get legal counsel. Once you have your documentation and you feel like you've found the vacation getaway you've always wanted to own, review the property documents with an attorney who is familiar with local laws governing fractional real estate.

When First Is Best

A development company offering its *first* fractional property actually may represent a tremendous purchasing opportunity for you. While fractional ownership is still a relatively new concept, it is already drawing in well-established real estate experts, commercial and residential developers, and hospitality companies that recognize the potential of fractional ownership and want to help people like you make the dream of second homeownership come true.

Although it warrants some additional due diligence, purchasing from a smaller, up-and-coming development company has its advantages. The most important benefit is *price performance*. Generally, you can get more for your investment with smaller and/or first-time developers. They often pay more attention to detail and offer premium amenities and services because it is their first project and they are keen to make their mark. Typically, they go the extra mile to ensure customer satisfaction and success.

THE EIGHT STEPS TO DUE DILIGENCE

Here are the *eight steps to due diligence* that determine whether a fractional property is right for you. They cover the elements you need to know to be in the know, ensuring that you've made an informed choice.

Step 1: Know the Developer

When considering a deluxe fractional property, learn all that you can about the people behind the scenes, including the developer of the fractional real estate property itself and the team of people who oversee the day-to-day operations. Sometimes these functions will involve two or more entities; sometimes one company will act as developer and operations manager.

Development companies can range in size. You will find that although some developers do not have the big name recognition, they still offer the high-end luxury accommodations, quality services, and desirable élan of a five-star resort hotel—without the exorbitant price that comes with the premium brand. Smaller developers offer you more personalized service and flexibility and often that feeling of owning your own private sanctuary.

Here are some of the questions you should ask about the *developer*:

- What is the developer's background, and what is their experience? Have they built luxury resorts? Have they built other fractional resorts?
- What other projects has the developer done? Ask for references.

- Is the developer familiar with the location of the property—including the geographic location, the culture, and the business workings of the area? Has the developer worked in the area before? Do they understand the unique requirements of developing in that location?

- Who is the developer working with to ensure the level of luxury amenities and services I want?

- Has the developer missed any sales or construction milestones in previous projects?

- Have there ever been any complaints or legal actions filed against the developer for any reason, such as for breach of contract, nonpayment, or fraudulent sales practices?

When Paradise Is Under Construction

Because fractional property development is emerging rapidly around the world, you will find wonderful shared-ownership opportunities in developments that are either under construction or yet to be developed. If you are pursuing a "paradise in progress," increased due diligence is critical.

As a perspective owner, you should have an experienced attorney review all documents to ensure that they conform to local laws that govern fractional real estate. Ask additional questions about the developer and their level of experience, completed projects, and problems or legal troubles they may have had.

Understand the timeline for development of the property and all associated amenities. Know your rights if the project is delayed or doesn't get built and what options you have for cancellation.

Talk to owners of other properties the developer has built. Above all, go with your gut. I put a lot of stock in human intuition. If it seems too good to be true, or if the promises made by the sales team or the developer strike you as unrealistic, and you get that nagging doubt in the pit of your stomach, listen to it and move on.

Step 2: Know the Management Team

You'll also want to have a clear sense of the companies who operate and maintain your fractional development. These are the people who are in charge of the care of your property and the quality of your experience as a shareholder. Because they hold the ultimate responsibility for your satisfaction as a fractional property owner, you need to make sure that they are people with whom you can easily communicate and trust.

Here are some of the questions you should ask about the *management team:*

- What management company will be in charge of daily operations and maintenance? What is their experience with this type of property management?
- Are there other hospitality companies that will be serving the fractional homeowners?
- Is there a board of directors or advisory board, and who sits on that board? Do shareowners represent a percentage of the board membership?
- Is there a relationship between the developer and the management company?
- How are disputes resolved between shareowners and the management company?
- Are there any conditions under which a shareowner would be forced to sell?
- What is the management fee paid to the management company?
- Will audited financial statements be made available to shareowners?

Step 3: Know Your Ownership Rights

As a fractional homeowner, you are the deeded shareowner of a particular residential condominium, townhouse, or single-family home, with the right to use your fractional vacation home—with all its amenities—for a designated number of days, weeks, or months per year.

The following questions will help you to explore whether the property you are interested in is indeed a true fractional and whether the purchase will meet your expectations as a deeded owner. Ask these types of questions about your *ownership rights:*

- As an owner, will I receive a recorded deed and title insurance?
- What is the profile of a typical owner?
- What are the available share percentages, and how many days of use am I guaranteed each year?
- How many shareholders are planned for my fractional second home, and how many shares are currently sold?
- What was the previous year's occupancy rate for the entire development?
- What are the current occupancy rates at comparable units? What can I realistically expect?
- What is the insurance coverage for common areas?
- Is there an official rules and regulations policy that I can review prior to purchase?
- Are there guidelines and regulations available for dress code, guests, entertaining, children, pets, noise, custom decor, etc.?
- What are the security arrangements?
- How much parking is allocated to each unit? Are additional spaces available? What are the terms?

> **At Home in Oregon**
>
> If you are looking for arts, culture, and grand es-
> capes to the great outdoors to kayak, fish, ski, and
> enjoy nature, Oregon has many exciting fractional
> developments for you to consider. Stylish urban de-
> velopments give you access to beautiful museums,
> stores, and the dazzling nightlife of Portland and
> Bend. Avid fans of the great outdoors are buying off-
> the-beaten-path resort fractional properties so that
> they can enjoy winter sports on beautiful Mt. Bache-
> lor, oceanfront living along Oregon's dramatic coast-
> line, river rafting and kayaking on the Columbia
> River, and exploring extensive state-protected wilder-
> ness areas with miles of hiking trails.
>
> Oregon is experiencing a wave of fractional home-
> buyers, and these buyers are folks like you—people
> ready to start living the good life now in their slice of
> paradise.

Step 4: Know Your Usage Plan

There is a vast array of usage plans available with fractional properties, with variances depending on such factors as high seasons versus rainy seasons, driving versus flying markets, and the most desirable dates, such as the Fourth of July, Thanksgiving, and the December holidays.

Fixed time gives you the comfort and convenience of

knowing your beachfront condo in Mexico is available to you the same weeks or months every year. For example, you know that the month of January is all yours, and you can rest easy that your vacation home will be there waiting for you—every January—with open arms.

Other plans use a *rotating calendar*, and your allotted time will rotate forward on the calendar on a predetermined basis every year. For example, if you are the owner of 1/12 share of a fabulous ski-in, ski-out fractional property in Telluride, a rotating calendar may have you using your vacation home the first week of each quarter in year one, the second week of each quarter in year two, and so on.

Other plans, such as *rotating priorities*, allow you to reserve new dates of stay every year. Here, you are able to reserve some of your allotted time during peak seasons, and if there are duplicate requests for a certain week, a rotating priority system comes into play. The first year, Owner A may get the first choice for, say, the first week of February. In year two, Owner A drops to the bottom of the list, and Owner B will get first dibs on that week. The rest of your ownership time then is placed in an as-available pool.

There are *hybrid* plans that are a combination of different types of usage plans. For instance, some of your time may be fixed and some may rotate or be on an as-available basis. In general, the more flexible the usage plan, the less available the most highly desirable timeslots may be. Conversely, the more fixed the plan (such as March every year), the less flexibility you have to change your month in a given year. The important thing to keep in mind is whether the usage plan fits *your* lifestyle and schedule.

Here are some essential questions regarding *usage plans:*

- What is the process for guaranteed and space-available usage? Is it a fixed or rotating schedule?
- Do I stay in the same unit each time, or is my unit floating?
- How are the seasons defined?
- How will occupancy be allocated between shareholders during peak season or major holidays?
- Do any blackout dates apply?
- Are there minimum or maximum stays?
- Is there a fixed weekday for arrival and check-out?
- Is there time set aside for annual maintenance of the unit?
- When do I get to select my dates of stay each year, and how does the reservation system work?
- Am I allowed to swap dates with another shareowner, or must I go through the established reservation system?
- Are there any restrictions regarding allowing my family or my guests to use my fractional vacation home when I am not present?

Step 5: Know Your Accommodations

The typical layout for a deluxe fractional resort vacation home or condo will include one to four bedrooms, a full modern kitchen, one or more private bathrooms, an office/study, and well-appointed living areas. Square footage can range from a 500-square-foot studio to 3,500+-square-foot residences. The current average fractional resort home generously measures about 1,750 square feet. Of course, the size of your most desirable slice of paradise will depend on your personal needs.

Fractional homeownership is all about high-style accommodations and a maintenance-free lifestyle. I recommend that you walk through your unit and take the time to imagine what it would be like to live there. See yourself awakening in your bedroom and then sipping your morning coffee in the kitchen. Take a seat in the living room and take in the beautiful vista. Look around and picture your family or guests enjoying a delicious meal at the dining room table.

Here are important questions to ask when you *try on a fractional property for size:*

- What is the square footage of my fractional property? How many bedrooms, bathrooms, etc.? Is a floor plan available?

- Assuming my accommodations will be furnished, what is the style of furniture and quality of the materials used? What color schemes are available? Are there alternative furnishings, color schemes, etc. from which I can choose? (If you have special needs, be sure to ask if they can be accommodated.)

- How will my furnishings be cared for and maintained, and how often will they be replaced? How will replacement be funded?

- How often will housekeeping clean my vacation home while I am there? Can I request more frequent housekeeping services?

- Are there covenants, conditions, and restrictions (CC's and R's) outlining what can and cannot be done with regard to my property, my neighbors' property, and the common areas?

- What do I need to do if I have a maintenance problem in my unit, such as a broken disposal or dishwasher? Are these kinds of services included in my assessment?

- Is smoking permitted in my residence? In the common areas?

- Are pets permitted in my residence? Are pets allowed on the premises? Are there restrictions?

Step 6: Know Your Amenities and Services

You've probably stayed at some of the most wonderful resort hotels in the world, paying top dollar for access to the amenities and services they offer. One phone call brings you towels or champagne and caviar. If you stay at a luxury brand hotel in Aruba, you usually can expect the same high level of service at their hotel in Boston.

Ask yourself what kind of pampering and pleasurable experience you want in a shared-ownership property, and then see how the development measures up to your wish list. At some fractional projects, separate fees may be assessed on a per-use basis for certain amenities or services.

Here are some of the questions you'll want to ask when exploring a fractional property's *amenities and services:*

- Is there a list of the full range of services and amenities available?

- Who actually owns the development's common-area amenities? If the amenities are subject to change, who makes the decision to change them and under what circumstances? How will I be notified of changes? Am I able to contest a change or to request special amenities?

- Do nonowners have the right to use the amenities (e.g., use the pool or private beach)? How is that usage monitored?

- What services can I expect as a shareowner? Does the development offer concierge services, valet services, housekeeping, transportation services, welcome/gift baskets, shopping services, pet-care services, an in-house chef, and other services on your wish list?

- Are there secure storage facilities for my skis, sporting gear, bikes, and other personal items? Will I be assigned a private, locked storage area, or will my items be locked in a common storage facility? Who will have keys?

- What is the check-in/check-out process for this development?

- Before I arrive, will my stored personal items be unpacked for me? Will they be stored away after departure?

- Can I have my own vehicle on the premises? Is secure parking available? Are there reliable, easily accessible automotive services?

- Are there any additional fees that I'll pay for the use of any of the amenities or services? Is a price list available?

- What are the specific terms for usage, guaranteed access, and guest privileges (e.g., greens fees, tee times, and health club visits)?

- Is there a list of commonly used nearby attractions and their fees? Are discounts available?

- Are there usage restrictions or surcharges for unaccompanied guests?

- Are memberships to private clubs available?

- Does the development offer access to an exchange program? If the answer is yes, is membership optional, or is it mandatory and folded into the ownership structure? What are the fees to participate?

Step 7: Know Your Financing Options

Before you purchase your fractional property, make sure that you are crystal clear about two significant factors—the options you'll have when it comes to financing your purchase and the fees you will pay as a shareowner of your resort property.

Banks and mortgage loan companies are beginning to treat fractional home purchases as they would the purchase of a wholly owned second home. It is also increasingly common for fractional vacation home purchasers to use home-equity lines of credit on their primary residences to secure their fractional second home. You also may be able to find independent methods of financing depending on your personal situation.

When you do decide to buy your dream vacation fractional, you will pay the one-time purchase price and then be responsible for yearly assessment or maintenance fees. These assessment fees cover the expenses of operating and maintaining your fractional property and any common areas and are costs often divided evenly among all the shareowners of a select property.

Here are some of the questions you'll want to ask concerning the *purchasing process:*

- Is a written description of the purchase process available?
- What is the purchase price of the fractional property, and what closing costs will I be responsible for?

- Is financing available from the developer? If so, what are the terms I can expect?

- When I make my downpayment, does the developer have any escrow arrangements or other financial assurances that protect my initial deposit?

- Under what terms is my deposit refundable?

- What is the estimated annual maintenance fee, and what does this specifically cover?

- What are the recurring maintenance fees? What are the anticipated annual increases in these fees? Are the fee increases capped?

- What are my cancellation rights?

Step 8: Know Your Investment

Most fractional homeowners buy their slice of paradise for personal use, as a place where they can relax in plush accommodations, ski, sail, walk, shop, and sample the local flavor to their heart's content. This *should* be the primary purpose of your purchase. However, some of you may be interested in other potential benefits, such as generating rental income and equity for resale.

If you are seriously interested in renting out your fractional property, you obviously will need to find out if the rules and regulations allow for rentals and if there are any restrictions. Do your homework! Understand the rental and occupancy rates in your market, and make sure that you have realistic expectations regarding what you'll be able to rent your property for and how often. You also can inquire as to whether your management company will assist in renting your property and, if so, what they charge.

As a deeded fractional shareowner, you are allowed to sell your fractional vacation home, just as you can sell your primary residence or a vacation home for which you are sole owner. Before you sell, however, you need to know whether your buyer will retain the same usage rights and privileges that you have enjoyed as the original purchaser. Most important, if resale is an important consideration in your decision, you should do your due diligence as to whether the market for your fractional property is soft or saturated, which could have an impact on resale opportunity and price.

Here are some important questions concerning the *rental* or *resale* of your fractional property, and you should make sure that you receive the answers in writing:

- Am I permitted to rent my property, and if so, what are the restrictions?

- Do I assist in the rental process? What is the fee or revenue split?

- Are there any fees or restrictions with the resale of my fractional property? If fees are involved, who is responsible for payment?

- Does the developer have a right of first refusal if I want to sell my ownership share?

- Does the buyer of my fractional property retain the same rights and privileges that I have had as the original purchaser?

- Have any units been resold by shareowners? Why did they sell? What was the appreciation?

BE IN THE KNOW

If you follow the suggested guidelines and ask the questions suggested here, you can rest assured that you will make an informed decision that will guarantee you years of enjoyment in your slice of paradise. The list of questions in this chapter, while not all-inclusive, is certainly comprehensive. For your convenience, I've made it available to you as a downloadable file on my website. Just go to *www.paradise bytheslicethebook.com* to download a copy. If you have additional questions, you also can feel free to contact me through the website or at *info@paradisebytheslicethe book.com*.

CHAPTER 6

Finding Your Slice in Foreign Lands

I f you are seriously considering buying a property outside the United States, thoughtful due diligence will ensure that your experience of second homeownership meets your expectations of what you want and need when you are there.

I've told you about that magical "I could *live* here" moment that I experienced on that special beach in Cabo San Lucas. It was clear that the region met all my personal criteria as far as climate, comfort, personal needs, and interests. As a real estate professional with a large portfolio of real estate properties in the United States, doing my due diligence was second nature. What wasn't as immediately clear was how to go about buying property in a foreign country. As an American citizen, was I actually permitted to own property in Mexico? And was it was a safe investment?

By the time I'd finished doing my extensive research, I knew that my dream of vacation homeownership in Cabo San Lucas would come true and that I not only could buy land on that untouched beach, but that I also could develop my own luxury fractional properties, a process that I describe in Chapter 7.

When approaching a property purchase in a foreign country, be it as near to the United States as Mexico or Canada or as distant as Europe or Africa, doing additional due diligence is an absolute necessity. You'll find that issues such as local government regulations on land ownership may be as unique to a country as its most alluring qualities.

As I've mentioned, your search for that perfect slice of the pie should start on the Internet. There is a vast array of information available at your fingertips—and in the comfort of your living room. Once you have determined your dream location, travel there to check it out. Most fractional development companies will assist you both online and onsite with navigating around the local landscape, be it in Mexico, Europe, or Fiji.

Foreign homeownership also requires that you receive excellent legal advice before you sign any documents or put any money down. In this case, *excellent* means a lawyer experienced with the legal ins and outs of second homeownership in the country that you call paradise.

Getting Beyond the Romance

Having your due-diligence ducks in a row is especially crucial with foreign properties because it's easy to get carried away by the almost hypnotic effect of a location while you're there. This is how the time-share industry grew in leaps and bounds. Tourists got wrapped up in the romance of "being there" and didn't pay enough attention to the fine print.

The stirring memory of a romantic stay at a five-star hotel in Paris or Rome also may trigger a desire to make a long-distance purchase. Believe or not, people do buy fractional properties without ever having seen the development. My strong suggestion, however, is to make a visit and, if possible, stay for a week or more. Get to know the locals, experience the climate, explore the terrain, and try something new. Who knew research could be such fun?

Then meet with the representatives from the development—and ask questions. Tour the property, and know exactly what you will get when you buy. Seek legal advice from an expert in the laws of that country. Along with doing your due diligence, follow your instincts and get a feel for what it would be like to "own" there. If you are anything like me, when it's right, it feels like *home*.

DOING YOUR PERSONAL DUE DILIGENCE

It's one thing to picture yourself enjoying your second home in Italy and another thing altogether to be there, be it for a few weeks or for months a year. Your fractional property—with its exceptional location, high level of service and amenities, and staff people who speak your language—will meet your needs while you're onsite. But what happens when you decide to adventure outside those castle walls?

Foreign cultures and environs often introduce you to the new and unusual—which is delightful as long as it's not an unexpected shock to your lifestyle. The truth is that when it comes to convenience, choice, and comfort, the United States is second to none. There really is no place like home.

In the United States, you can find convenience stores, gas stations, ATMs, restaurants, bars, and drug stores open twenty-four hours a day, 365 days a year. There is always a cab available at 2 a.m. in New York. When you switch on the radio or widescreen television in Aspen, the programs are for the most part in English. Your health insurance covers you in all fifty states. There are banks in every town, and the cash you carry in your wallet in Lake Tahoe is the same cash they'll accept in Fort Lauderdale.

Living north or south of the border or overseas can be surprisingly different from what you've come to know and expect in the United States. One of my partners is fond of saying, "The only thing that stays the same in Mexico is that everything is different." This new adventure to second homeownership is part of the *joy*—as long as you are prepared in advance.

You may be ready to buy a fractional vacation home in Florence or Cancun because each time you've visited there, you've felt the magic like I did! Are you ready to speak Italian or Spanish? Are you comfortable with the culture of the country? Do you know how the health care system works? Do you know how to get around from point A to point B and what to expect as far as auto insurance?

To find a reliable tour guide who speaks English as well as the local language typically takes just a phone call to the concierge of your fractional development, but there will be times when you'll want to strike out on your own. That's when you'll want to be able to converse comfortably with vendors at the artisan market or with the saleswoman in the fabulous Left Bank boutique—and that can mean learning a new language. And while you're shopping, you'll need to know the local currency, be it euros, pesos, or the South African rand.

Cultural differences also can vary widely from country to country. There are communities where modes of dress may be strictly dictated or where women traveling alone are frowned on. Businesses close up shop on different national and religious holidays, meal times may differ significantly, and some towns shut down daily for three-hour siestas.

Developments in some of the Central and South American countries offer the height of luxury living amid the lush rain forests, yet extreme poverty in the larger cities is still acutely apparent. Haggling about price is completely natural in some countries, whereas other places have two accepted pricing structures for products and services—one for the native people and a second one for the outsiders.

Getting around by car also may not be for the faint of heart because unpaved roads and poor signage can present a major challenge. While a U.S. driver's license is honored throughout most of the civilized world, you'll want to make sure that you know what is legally required in the country you choose for your fractional home, as well as what auto insurance best protects you in case of an accident.

Health care is another key consideration. Where is the closest hospital to your vacation home, and what is the quality of care? What happens if you get a toothache at midnight? Are there personnel onsite who are trained in first aid and CPR? Most countries offer health care that meets or rivals what you find in American hospitals. But you can probably assume that your American health insurance policy will *not* cover you in a foreign country. Vacation home living in New Zealand now means that you'll need some kind of international health insurance. This is especially significant if you have special health care needs.

As you seriously consider buying a property outside the United States, explore the local culture, the lifestyle of people who live near or around your deluxe development, the types of foods they eat, the political climate, and the local view of foreign visitors. All of this adds to the pleasure of your purchase and the peace of mind you'll enjoy as you look out over the Alps or the Sea of Cortez and sigh, "Home at last!"

Dreaming of Dubai

Dubai is a place that stretches your imagination, much like the sand and crystal clear waters extend as far as the eye can see. Politically safe and full of opportunities for international travelers and investors alike, Dubai amazes visitors with its modern architecture, first-rate shopping centers, green parks, and rugged mountains—all in a rich, multicultural environment. Shared-ownership properties are already available here, and others will be opening their own luxurious fractional developments in Dubai soon.

Some fractional properties in Dubai are *mixed use,* and you'll find that large fractional projects around the world offer similar ownership models. A development will start with full ownership of the units and then move into fractional offerings. Mixed use is becoming the norm for new fractional projects offered by the larger brand developers because it satisfies the needs of their varied customers—full owners, fractional owners, and other guests.

INVESTING IN MEXICO

Mexico deserves some special attention in this chapter because of the exploding popularity of tourism and vacation homeownership there. The foresight and funding of the pro-U.S. Mexican government has made this wonderful neighbor to the south the fastest growing tourism market in Central America, with the communities of Puerto Vallarta and Cabo San Lucas as the growth leaders. While Mexico historically has depended on oil and gas revenues to fund its economy, a deteriorating industry infrastructure and depleting oil and gas reserves inspired the government to replace oil and gas as the chief source of revenue.

The result is Fonatour, a national agency focused only on tourism. Fonatour has the largest budget of Mexico's myriad governmental agencies, and its sole purpose is revenue growth through tourism. Of its multi-billion-dollar budget, 31 percent is earmarked for the southern Baja, Cabo San Lucas, and La Paz. Twenty-nine percent of the budget is allocated for the Mexican state of Nayarit, including Puerto Vallarta and other areas north. A full $2.3 billion—yes, that's *billion*—has already been invested in such vital necessities as major highways, state-of-the-art airports, marinas, and municipal roads. It's clear that Mexico is readying itself for continued growth in tourism and vacation homeownership. The focus is on *you*, and the country's investment is huge.

If I had to put the benefits of second homeownership in Mexico in one word, it would be *balance*. Everything about this amazing country points to enjoying life to the fullest, from water sports and archaeological sites to its beaches and the tranquil siestas every afternoon. The food, the music, the people, the weather, and the vast number of things to do are remarkable in themselves, and when you take into consideration that the cost of living is two-thirds of what it is in the United States, you're talking paradise! With fractional ownership, you can have the heavenly lifestyle when you want it and how often you choose, be it two weeks, one month, four months, or more each year.

YOUR LIFESTYLE IN MEXICO

With an average year-round temperature ranging between seventy-five and eighty-five degrees Fahrenheit and a very limited rainy season, your lifestyle in Mexico will include a warm, comfortable climate nearly every day of the year. This means that you can swim at all hours of the day and all year round. I love being able to walk outdoors in the evenings without wearing a coat or even a sweater. Sunset dinner on the beach, anyone? You can do that every evening. If you decide to dine out, you have your pick of high-end four-star restaurants, or you can take a tip from the locals and feast on a $4 dinner that includes your beer.

The Mexican lifestyle is relaxed and easy—ideal for recharging your inner "batteries" and quite a departure from the fast pace we typically experience in the United States. The Mexican people are open and friendly, taking life at a slower pace and upholding the age-old tradition of making your day, from generously inviting you to embrace their culture to sending you a smile and a cordial *"Buenos dias"* as you pass on the street.

The question, "What do you feel like doing today?" takes on new meaning in Mexico. In Cabo San Lucas, there is a full-service marina for deep sea fishing aficionados. Divers and snorkelers are just a short boat ride from the harbor to a spectacular underwater nature preserve. You have access to top-notch golf courses and tennis courts and endless sandy beaches for long, leisurely hikes—beaches kept free of overdevelopment by local regulations.

Puerto Vallarta, like Cabo San Lucas, offers the same relaxed pace, and you can go whale watching in the second largest bay in North America, hiking in the jungle, or dancing until dawn. Ixtapa is known for its virgin beaches and eco-tours to offshore islands, as well as lively evening entertainment in the wonderful downtown district.

When it comes to life in a laid-back paradise, Mexico offers you baby boomers looking to downsize and you retirees planning to purchase second homes just what you've been looking for—life on the beach! Add to this the fact that your fractional property is easily accessible by plane from most places in the United States, and you have a slice of paradise that is just a few short hours away from your family and friends.

YOUR INVESTMENT IN MEXICO

Keith and Tara had been traveling once a year to Mexico from their home in Philadelphia for over fifteen years, and they had seen resort hotels and exciting nightspots spring up in key areas along the Pacific coastline. The country never seemed to lose its magic for them, and they thought of the area surrounding Puerto Vallarta as their "second home" long before it became possible for them to consider buying property there.

Self-employed, with grown kids and a mortgage close to being paid off, the couple knew that they wanted to spend at least a month a year in their slice of paradise south of the U.S. border. It was the perfect spot for a winter getaway, where Tara could work on her paintings while Keith played golf or went deep sea fishing. Over the past fifteen years, it had been relatively easy to find a house to rent, but it was always a chore to lug down the sports gear and art supplies. Finding a house or apartment with Internet access also was a constant challenge because Keith needed to stay in touch with his international clients, even while on vacation.

The idea of buying a home in Mexico sounded exciting, but they had serious questions about the risks involved. Was it a safe financial investment? What would happen to their property the eleven months of the year that they were back in Philadelphia? What kind of fees and taxes would they have to pay? Could they actually own the property, or did they lease it from the government?

Fractional properties were plentiful pickings on the Internet, and they decided to contact a developer in Puerto Vallarta whose luxuriously furnished seaside fractional villas appeared to fit their needs. The substantial layout included three bedrooms, one of which could be converted easily into an art studio for Tara—when she wasn't on the veranda painting the amazing ocean view. There also was a perfect place in the sizable living room to comfortably tuck away a computer, and wireless Internet access meant that Keith could stay one click away from his customers at all times— even from his laptop on the beach.

The conversation with the sales office was illuminating to say the least. Not only was Mexico eagerly welcoming Americans interested in buying vacation homes there, the process was as safe as and certainly no more complicated than what they'd face buying a second home in Florida. The fractional development also offered the right-sized, right-priced 1/12 share they were looking for, securing their dream of one month a year in their slice of paradise, full equity for their share, and a management company protecting their investment during the long months they were away in Philadelphia.

Here's what you need to know about Mexico: Whether you are looking to buy a resort fractional property or to develop one or more properties like I am doing, Mexico is unquestionably a great place to invest because this country is experiencing tremendous appreciation. As I am writing this book, the real estate market in the United States is extremely soft. Cash flow from real estate is rare, and appreciation is exceptionally hard to find. In Mexico, it is quite the opposite. For instance, that rare beauty of a condo on the beach typically would cost about $500,000 to build and would sell for $800,000 to $1.2 million a unit. Buyers of these luxury homes are foreign tourists looking for second homes or vacation homes where they can spend extended periods of time lounging on the beach, playing golf to their heart's content, or reeling in that prized marlin. For them, it is about the experience, not the cost. By purchasing a property where you only pay for what you use, realizing the dream of owning one or more "second homes" in desirable resort areas easily becomes reality.

Mexico is a safe place, both for investment purposes and as a place to own your fractional vacation home. It used to be a scary prospect to purchase property or to live in a foreign country. Haven't we all heard some kind of horror story about a foreign government confiscating property, leaving the owner high and dry?

That was then, and this is now. In 1993, the Mexican government created the *fideocomiso system* of foreign property ownership. A *fideocomiso* is, in essence, a bank trust that holds the title to your property, much like a mortgage company in the United States holds your property when you carry a mortgage. The bank is the trustee, ensuring that there is proper title to the property, and title insurance is secured by a U.S. title insurance company. Imagine—the American title company for your luxurious Mexico fractional even may be the same title company that holds the title insurance on your primary residence in the United States.

You also can rest assured that the trust is a fifty-year, automatically renewable bank trust in which you have all the rights of ownership you've come to know and love. This means that your fractional property in Cabo San Lucas or Acapulco is yours to rent, to sell, and to leave to your heirs, just as you would as the owner of a vacation home in San Diego or South Beach. And in case you're curious, no owner, to my knowledge, has lost his or her property since the adoption of the *fideocomiso* system in Mexico.

YOUR HEALTHY LIFE IN MEXICO

As I've said, health care is a critical personal consideration if you are thinking about purchasing a second home in a foreign country. Fortunately, health care in Mexico is excellent because most Mexican physicians and dentists have received part of their training (and pursue ongoing training) in the United States and Europe.

The coastal beauties—Cabo San Lucas, Puerto Vallarta, and Ixtapa—have at least one superb hospital, staffed by English-speaking emergency care units, pharmacists, and skilled primary care physicians—many of whom still make house calls. In fact, you'll find at least one exceptional hospital in every midsize to large city in the country.

Other good news is that the cost of health care and prescription drugs is typically one-half of what you pay in the United States, which explains why many Americans are traveling to foreign countries like Mexico to receive medical and dental treatment! As a general rule before purchasing a fractional second home in any foreign country, if you have a serious medical condition, please investigate first whether your special needs can be met.

Finally, you may be wondering about crime. Although there are geographic pockets where crime has been an issue, in the larger, more populated or tourist-friendly Mexican locales where large developers are building luxury resorts, crime is quite rare. I have spent countless days over the past few years exploring Mexico's major cities, and I have always felt safe. If safety and security are important factors for you, you may want to focus on gated communities offering twenty-four-hour security, and you will have plenty of choices.

Once you start exploring Mexico as your slice of paradise, you will be entranced by its natural beauty, enchanted by the warm, friendly people, and amazed by the variety of experiences available to you. It's no wonder that Mexico is the destination of choice for American retirees and investors who are buying a second home outside the United States. It's close, easy to get to, and you can find luxurious private fractional communities in every phase of development, from those that are fully operational today to new vacation home wonderlands that are soon to be constructed.

It's a country truly overflowing with opportunity for the second homebuyer and the real estate developer.

GETTING TO YES

Going from "I could *live* here!" to "I am *going* to live here!" takes us all through some undiscovered territory, especially when considering a fractional property in a foreign land. One of my business partners is a great guy named Will Mattox, owner of Select Mexico Properties. Like me, he fell in love with Mexico. He not only took the leap to make this special country his second home, but he also has become a successful, enthusiastic real estate developer there. Will is an accomplished business coach and was my coach some years ago at Live Out Loud. Occasionally, Will and I find ourselves talking about the "tough stuff" in our business, such as the barriers people encounter when it comes to buying a vacation home in a foreign country.

One balmy afternoon in Cabo San Lucas, after a particularly productive meeting with our development team, we sat together at the local beach club taking in the view, sipping an ice-cold beer, and basking in the satisfaction that comes with saying yes to a great opportunity. We were chatting about our fractional project and the buyers whose lives would be enriched by the experience of owning the vacation homes we were developing. I knew that many prospective homeowners would see what we had to offer and jump at the chance to realize the dream. Who'd be crazy enough to say no to living in paradise? But, as an experienced real estate professional, I also knew that choosing a second home was often an emotional decision—one that forces us to come face to face with the fear of considering the unknown.

As Will and I sipped our beers and looked out over the Pacific Ocean, I thought about why some people were motivated to buy property in a foreign country while others never seemed to be able to take the leap. Many purchase a fractional property in an exotic location for the lifestyle benefits—the promise of what they'll feel and experience when they are there. Others are attracted to the fractional ownership investment opportunity. Sure, the location is heaven on earth, but what's the return on investment (ROI)? It's the voice of our inner analyst as it stares at the spreadsheet and says, "Show me the money!" And as much as any one of us would love to throw caution to the wind and follow our "just do it" impulses, our inner voice of reason also demands that an emotional choice make rational sense. This is what helped us to become successful in the first place! We have the financial solvency to buy a second home because we worked hard and made solid, informed choices. This is why this book emphasizes doing your due diligence.

However, even with a passionate calling to buy a second home and the willingness to do meticulous due diligence, some potential buyers find themselves stuck in some middle ground between the emotional pull of living the dream and the inner push for getting the facts. Owning a second home in Mexico feels right to you, and all the data you need to make it happen are available. But you just can't take that next step. Why does this happen?

Will has spent over eleven years as a business and real estate investment coach, supporting many people in their search for the lifestyle and investment benefits we have been discussing in this book. As we sat talking at that Cabo beach club, Will said that he had discovered that there are really only *two* reasons for the stalemate. And these two barriers to becoming a second homeowner in a foreign country are easy to understand and overcome.

"I'd live three months a year in Mexico (or Italy or Costa Rica) if I found the right property, but I just don't know what's available."

As Will put it to me, the first reason for the stalemate is: *"We don't know what we don't know."* If you know that you'd love to spend your winter months in Puerto Vallarta, but you don't have a direct point of contact there—like someone with a home there or a business partner—it's time to make use of the treasure trove of resources just waiting for you on the Internet. You'll find websites like mine (*www.paradisebytheslicethebook.com*) and active blogs where people share their insights and recommendations. Want to window shop the properties in your dream exotic location? You'll find listings with detailed descriptions and images. Need a good real estate agent or point person in Puerto Vallarta? You'll find him or her through testimonials and recommendations.

To move from *"I just don't know what's available"* to happy vacation homeowner in your favorite country outside your homeland is at your fingertips: Just turn on your computer. Or if you'd rather start with talking with someone who has walked in your shoes, feel free to contact me through my website, and I'll help guide you.

"I found what I want, and it's perfect. But I wonder if it's really a safe and smart choice."

You've found it—the slice of paradise in Cabo that seems just right for you. Your heart beats faster when you imagine yourself living there, and all the numbers add up to a good investment. But no matter how close you try to get to yes, *fear* keeps pulsing in your stomach.

This is the second reason people get stuck: *fear of the unknown*. We are all afraid of the unknown—afraid of any negative stories we may have heard, afraid of making a mistake that will cost us money, afraid of the strange language or the unfamiliar environment. Fear is a survival instinct and an asset in most situations. Fear keeps us from walking off a cliff! Maybe you even recall an instance when you ignored the fear throbbing in your gut, and the failure that resulted still haunts you.

Fear is a valuable inner warning system, but it isn't always indicating an imminent disaster. The truth is that more often than not your fear is telling you that you have some unanswered questions. Happily, there is a simple solution for calming the "fear of the unknown": Get the answers you need. Will gave me two valuable exercises for getting past the fear—no surprise to me because he is such a remarkable coach—and I heartily recommend that you use them.

First, think back to a scary choice you had to make, one in which you made your decision to proceed only after you got the answers you needed. For me, it was when I was faced with my first "century" bike ride. I was new on the cycling scene when my riding buddies suggested that we do a century and signed me up. One hundred miles on a bike! Were they kidding? I remember thinking, I have trouble driving a car 100 miles. How could I possibly ride a bicycle 100 miles? How could my body take what I calculated to be six to seven hours on a bike? What would I do for food and water? How would my legs, my back, my rear end go for that long without just giving out? I was terrified. I trained for that ride, and I did my research on centuries. I finished that century tired, but let me tell you, it was a thrill of a lifetime. Looking back on it now, and after going on to complete countless other centuries, I am amazed that fear of the unknown almost prevented me from one of the purest joys of my life.

Second, it's one thing to be afraid of the dark and another to be afraid because you are "in the dark." Get a piece of paper or get on your computer, and make a list of every question you have about the property you'd like to buy and what's holding you back. Go back to Chapter 5 and reread some of the questions available there. Then identify every fear that's talking to you. When you are done, go back to the top of list and identify the person who has the answer you need to each question. Maybe each item on the list will have "Contact Janet" next to it. That's' okay. I'll help you get your answers. Finally, contact the people on the list, and get every answer until you feel that you are making an informed decision. You still may have some butterflies when you sign on the dotted line, but chances are those final flutters will be more about the excitement that comes with getting to yes!

DEVELOPING FRACTIONAL PROPERTIES

For those of you interested in exploring the role of fractional property developer, Chapter 7 is for you. It's great reading for everyone, but I've specifically packaged the information and experience I've collected over my years as a developer for those of you who share my passion for enabling people to realize their dreams through luxury resort homeownership.

CHAPTER 7

Development in Paradise

Whether you are an experienced real estate developer or a fellow entrepreneur curious about what it would take to develop a fabulous fractional property, going from idea to execution means doing in-depth research.

As a passionate entrepreneur with experience in the real estate industry and second homeownership, the move into fractional real estate development came naturally to me. The benefits to my shareowners were clear and significant—deeded homeownership of a slice of paradise with all the pluses of luxury resort living without the pleasure-depleting minuses, such as do-it-yourself home maintenance and a huge price tag.

I also knew that becoming a developer of a deluxe fractional property held great potential for me, including both personal growth and financial gain. Because I'm an entrepreneur at heart, it was no surprise when my "I could *live* here!" moment in Cabo San Lucas quickly evolved into a compelling what-if proposition—"What if I developed my own property here?"

I'll never forget the day I drove out from Cabo San Lucas to explore land I'd learned was available for development. As I drove north from Cabo with the man who soon would become our developer, my partner and I experienced Baja California Sur. To the right we saw the sweeping panoramic view of the desert, framed in the distance by the majestic 6,000-foot Sierra de la Laguna Mountain Range. To our right was the Pacific Ocean in all its beauty and glory.

We were in the market to buy land, and our new-found friend commented, "You don't know how hard we worked to put that ocean out there for you." To this day we still laugh at that.

When we reached Cerritos Beach, I was in awe. A famous surfer beach, it is breathtakingly beautiful and untouched—a true oasis, if you know where to find it. Stretching for miles, the white sand and cool, blue ocean blew me away. We walked from a point just above the beach to the available lot. As we stood on the bluff overlooking the water only feet away, I knew that this was the place. I would own property on that beach. I would build a luxury resort for others to enjoy. I had found my dream, and I would share that dream with others.

That was just the beginning. On my next trip to the area, I visited Tequila Ranch, which is just a short distance from Cerritos Beach. Tequila Ranch is an exclusive gated private resort featuring a tequila distillery. But it's not just any distillery! This one is built in the likeness of the old José Cuervo distillery and features a gourmet restaurant overlooking the ocean. The restaurant itself serves organic produce grown in the neighboring town of Pescadero, a lush oasis in the middle of the Baja desert known for its production of organic fruits and vegetables.

Once again, my partner and I were just blown away—and perhaps a little *carried* away, because we bought three lots in the Tequila Ranch development. Our plan for our fractional villa project was born. My partner and I closed the deal in the airport bar before heading back home. I remember that the flight home was one of those "dream come true" moments that I'll never forget. I gazed out the window of that plane thinking, "Somebody pinch me. . . . "

Pescadero and Cerritos Beach are just thirty-five miles from the popular town of Cabo San Lucas, and they are among those rare, hidden treasures that still can be found in Mexico. Boasting one of the only swimmable beaches on the Pacific side, this area is a geographic gem that has yet to be explored by most tourists, let alone developed. One of the things I love most about this particular area is its proximity to the booming, lively town of Cabo while being off the beaten track with a quiet, tranquil, and exclusive feel to it.

A scant six miles away is the town of Todos Santos. Known for its local art galleries and great fishing and home of the famous Hotel California, this quaint fishing village is a popular hangout for visiting artists and tourists alike, who go there to capture the local color and then feast on fresh-fish tacos and icy cold Mexican beer.

During the first year of ownership in Tequila Ranch, as we raised capital, the land continued to appreciate at a rapid rate as we watched the infrastructure of water, power, roads, and more come to our properties. In a little over a year, the land itself had tripled in value. Is that good news? Yes! Is that typical? Perhaps not, but opportunities like this do exist.

I'd like to say that it was my great foresight and knowledge of real estate that was responsible for our investing in this area of Mexico. While partly true, truth be told, the credit goes to the great team I had assembled to purchase and develop the resort of my dreams. You see, so many of us believe that we can do it all and that we need to control it all. For me, my team of experts—people in fields where I was a novice—gave me the confidence to stretch beyond what I could do alone. Finding the right property is very much a key to a successful fractional project, but having the right team is equally important. Finding *both* is the key to becoming a successful fractional property developer.

How do you find the right property and the right team? First, you need to be open to finding them. Then you do extensive research. The key to your success as a fractional developer depends on your focus on developer *due diligence.*

FINDING PROPERTIES WITH REAL POTENTIAL

If you are already a developer of full-ownership properties, you are already way ahead of the game, but don't fool yourself into believing that full ownership and fractional ownership are the same. The target market, although similar, is not the same. The product itself is very different. With fractional ownership, it is all about the finishes, the amenities, and the owner experience, so the way you market your development is very different. The sales process is different; your salespeople will need different skills because there are anywhere from four to thirteen more units to sell versus one with full ownership.

I know of developers who have enthusiastically jumped into the world of fractionals with both feet. They bought a beautiful property and poured lots of money into, getting it ready for those beachcombers or ski bunnies. Then nobody showed for the party—or they went to different parties—as the developer paced the premises for months wondering what went wrong.

If you are brand new to the world of fractional development, my recommendation is to find someone already doing what you want to do. Developing a fractional project is much more complicated than full-ownership development. Never fear, help is on the way! Companies such as Ragatz Associates, with their comprehensive feasibility studies, can save you time and money by advising you regarding your plans to develop a property as a fractional.

A feasibility study will cover market research analysis and indicate who your target buying group is and how best to reach them. It also will tell you what roadblocks you could run into—and sometimes a *roadblock* is a literal term. Companies such as Ragatz Associates are experts in providing the kind of detailed research you need for your market. Believe me, the upfront investment will clarify whether your potential property fits the profile of a paradise or whether the whole process will turn out to be a living hell.

The first step is finding that certain location that you know is a Mecca for vacationers. You've been there and perhaps even had your own "I could *live* here!" moment. Once you've found it, it's time to start (or continue, as the case may be) to build your team. Do you need to secure financing, commercial or private equity? Who do you need on your team to help with that? Once you have secured the property through an option or a purchase, does it need to be rezoned?

Grading of the property comes next, and then design of the physical site and individual units. Once defined, the project must get the proper entitlements. Then there are the ever-important services and amenities that can make or break your project. There is a sales and marketing strategy to plan and implement. Sales need to be made, staff needs to be hired and trained, units need to be furnished, legal documents need to be drawn up, usage plans need to be determined, a rules and regulations document needs to be created, and on and on.

Before this all starts to seem overwhelming, let's take a closer look at the broad-stroke realities of the fractional development process. As you read, it will become crystal clear why this "homework" is necessary and why it takes a team to make it all happen.

KNOW YOUR MARKET

For a second homebuyer, *location* is all about a special place where he or she can experience the finest that resort vacation homeownership can offer. It's the perfect home away from home, the beach is right outside the front door, and golf or fishing is readily accessible, as is the amazing gourmet meal afterward. It's the ease of arriving at your destination and leaving all worries and responsibilities behind. It's a place you can't wait to return to time after time; perhaps it's where you eventually retire.

For the developer, location starts with that spot on the map. Governing that spot are shared-ownership laws and state and local regulations. If your spot on the map is in a foreign country, there may be even stricter laws overseeing new development. Remember what I said about Bermuda in Chapter 3? Bermuda has looser laws regarding fractional ownership for the unit buyer, but this idyllic island has a "locals first" law in place so that native islanders can purchase affordable homes. This affects what land you can buy, and in some places, available property is at a premium.

Beachfront property is often earmarked for preservation, limiting overdevelopment, and your plan for private beach access for your owners also may be thwarted if public access is required. In some instances, ecological concerns and vigilant oversight of marine, desert, forest, and/or mountain wilderness areas could curtail development, especially where plant and animal species are protected by law.

Once you've cleared any legal or regulatory barriers to building and/or developing a fractional property, a vital next step has to do with infrastructure. Before I purchased the Tequila Ranch properties, I had already verified that there would be paved access roads to my property, as well as a nearby water treatment plant, electricity, and even cellular and high-speed digital signals. This is obviously less of a concern in developed primary markets and urban areas, where the infrastructure is already in place. It is, however, an important part of your due diligence if your property is off the beaten track—which will become more prevalent as prime resort markets become more and more saturated.

Selecting Secondary Markets

In the real estate world, there are primary markets and secondary markets. A primary market already may be saturated with hotels, timeshare developments, and second home communities. Even if you find a property—say, a development open to conversion—you need to know if the market can bear another resort property. If your choice is a secondary market, is it a desirable market for your target share-owners? What is the market for full ownership? If the market is weak for full ownership, selling fractional ownership will be difficult. Will fractional ownership actually *sell* there?

Whether your potential market is considered primary or secondary, learn as much as you can about it. Research hotel vacancy rates, cost per night, and high seasons and off-seasons. Check out the airports for the frequency of flights and where inbound flights originate. Look at the unemployment rates and which businesses are local. What is the plan for enticing more companies into the market, or are companies leaving this market? Find out about the rental market—is it strong, weak, getting better, or declining? And of course, look into the local real estate market. Is it an appreciating market? What is the average time on the market for similar properties?

These questions are critical to being able to clearly discern whether or not a potential market is optimal for the success of your fractional development both in the short term and in the long term.

THAT ALL-IMPORTANT LOCAL CONNECTION

If you live in Chicago and plan to develop a deluxe fractional property, whether it's in Florida or in a foreign country, you have to understand how your market *works* so that you can get your development built. You need to learn how the local zoning laws and permit processes work, how to find and manage the right contractors, and who the local people and businesses are that will be important to your business now and in the future.

If you are not local and don't have the connections you need to get things done, consider finding someone local and adding him or her to your team. I can't tell you how many times I've talked to developers who have purchased property in prime locations and then struggled with getting their projects built because they didn't have the local connections needed to get them done.

For my Mexico projects, I've partnered with a long-time local resident and development professional who knows the ins and outs of the entire area. Instead of trying to absorb the lay of the land on my own, I have a valuable point person who knows from personal experience what to expect at each step of the way. He knows how to streamline processes and build the relationships required for the success of our projects. His insider knowledge is worth its weight in gold, and it is necessary to help ensure that there's complete satisfaction across the board—for you, for the project, and for your future shareowners.

A Word on Partners

Partners, in the purest sense of the word, are team members who have an equity interest in the project. Most of the members of my team are not actual equity partners, but professionals with the skills we need to make the project successful. They are team members who are hired and paid by the hour for their services.

Partners are folks who share in the risks and rewards inherent in any kind of major project. Partners can bring expertise, money, credit, "sweat equity," and other forms of contribution to the partnership. This means that a partnership or joint venture is a legal relationship and should be in the form of a legal and binding agreement signed by all parties.

As my good friend Loral is fond of saying, "Plan your divorce while you are still in love." Document your exit strategy! What happens if one of the partners wants out? Can you vote a partner out? What happens (God forbid) if one of the partners passes away?

I've learned a valuable lesson on partnerships, and I learned it the hard and painful (and expensive) way. Never partner with someone who doesn't share your values. Follow your intuition, even if it means walking away from what, at the time, seems like the best deal ever.

KNOW YOUR BUYER

Over the next two decades, demand for luxury vacation homeownership is expected to skyrocket as the nineteen million baby boomers in the United States reach their peak earning potential, transition to empty nesters, look with anticipation to their retirement years, and see substantial financial gain through inheritance. Surely the $2.3 billion spent on fractional homeownership and new developments in 2007 will only continue to grow!

Financing Your Fractional Development

The real estate capital markets in the United States are currently experiencing a significant slowdown. There are severe liquidity constraints on funding both for full-use properties and for fractional projects. The fractional industry itself is also facing its own challenges because the market has been weakened by the condo market and the fact that inexperienced lenders are avoiding this sector. However, financing for fractional projects is available!

Here is what lenders will expect from you:

- A strong target market—what socioeconomic group and from where?
- Resalability of property
- Amenity appeal
- Usage plans and program details
- Downpayments of 20 to 30 percent

- Presales—sometimes up to as much as 50 percent
- Developer experience (prior fractional sales)

Remember too that financing is often available for projects directly from the developer. It is often a more cost-effective form of financing because it typically doesn't require the need for extensive documentation. However, you can expect that collateral may be required, such as securing the financing through the equity of your primary residence.

Here is what you can expect from the financing process:

- It will take a long time, so engage prospective financing options early.
- You will need presales.
- It will cost you more than financing a wholly owned property.
- Full documentation will be needed, which includes not only your financials but also the plan for the resort, including site plans, floor plans, common-area amenities, etc.

You are going to want to look for companies that specialize in financing for fractional projects. More information and assistance are available on my website, *www.paradisebytheslicethebook.com*.

Turning *potential* into a successful business reality goes beyond the proverbial "build it and they will come" approach. You need to know who is buying second homes in your market, what they are paying, how often they travel there, and how long they stay. This can start with learning who is choosing this place as their vacation destination. One of the ways I have identified my target buyers is quite simple: Check out the flights into your market, and find out where they originate. If your development will be in Central America, for example, you may discover that vacation travelers come not only from the United States but also from Europe or Australia. If your market is a driving market, find out where people are traveling from and how far they typically drive to get to your destination.

Study your market, and learn about the demographics of the people who select your area from the myriad slices of paradise available. Also be sure to talk with other established fractional developers in your market to discern what is selling and what isn't. Do what I did and visit every currently-for-sale fractional and timeshare available in the area. Yes, I said *timeshare* because I have learned a lot by studying what they have to offer in Cabo—in my own backyard, so to speak.

You might want to go as far as to commission a study of the market. Differing from a fractional feasibility study, this type of study covers the demographics of the region. Talk to other developers about what works best as far as the usage plan. If your target shareowner drives to your area several times a year to ski and walk the mountain trails, your usage plan will be different from that for a buyer who flies in and spends four to eight weeks at a time relaxing in his or her second home.

You'll also want to note that many large fractional projects start with full ownership and piggyback off full ownership to eventually include fractionals. This is referred to as *mixed use* and is becoming more of the norm for fractional projects offered by the larger brand developers.

KNOW YOUR BUSINESS

As a fractional property developer, you enter the exciting world of the hospitality industry. Your buyer will have his or her choice of amazing resort hotels, luxurious rental properties, long-established timeshares, and even local second homes for sale or rent. Your key differentiator is that fractional ownership offers what the "competition" cannot come close to providing—the *best* features and benefits that each has to offer in one all-inclusive package.

Fractional ownership gives your buyer deeded title, equity, and flexible access to a deluxe, cost-effective, beautifully furnished, maintenance-free slice of paradise loaded with the most desirable amenities and services. This is the promise of fractional ownership, and this is what your development must deliver.

There are obstacles to converting a resort-destination traveler into a resort fractional homeowner. The one that comes up time and again is, as I've mentioned, that most potential buyers do not have a clear picture of fractional ownership. They commonly confuse *fractional ownership* with timeshare "ownership," which is like confusing a diamond with a cubic zirconium. Lovely, yes. As intrinsically valuable, no.

This means that knowing the hospitality industry inside and out is imperative. If you don't know it, partner with someone who does. Pay special attention to this area because services and the levels of amenities are the critical factors that will differentiate your project from others on the market. Once you know your market and your target fractional homebuyer, you need to know how to best communicate with your future shareowners and how to make the purchasing process as seamless and pleasurable as possible.

SALES AND MARKETING OF YOUR FRACTIONAL PROPERTY

You've done your due diligence, found the property, understand your market, know your target buyer, and are ready to move into marketing and sales. Begin this action step by adding an attorney experienced in fractional ownership to draw up your legal documents and contracts. This includes sales contracts, usage plans, and rules and regulations that determine how the property can be used.

Your marketing plan should be multipronged and may include direct mail, telemarketing, advertising in leading travel magazines and local periodicals, printing high-end brochures to place in key restaurant kiosks, or renting prime billboard space along the road from the airport. An attractive, information-rich website, which includes virtual tours, is a must because potential buyers of luxury fractional properties are the affluent and superaffluent, and they typically use the Internet to research pretty much everything they need, from clothes to hillside cottages in the British Isles. In general, expect to spend between 20 and 30 percent of your overall budget on marketing and sales.

If your development is in the preconstruction phase, you will want to enable potential buyers to imagine themselves there. Be forewarned: From my experience, it is much more difficult to sell fractional units without a luxuriously finished and accommodated model unit, so anything you can do to enable the emotions of the buyer, do it. At a minimum, you will need artistic renderings of floor plans and site maps and a virtual tour that allows them to visualize themselves there.

Since most shareowners make a decision to purchase a deluxe fractional unit when they are on location at the development, you'll want to ensure a positive, provocative, and informative sales experience that begins *before* the buyer arrives and continues *after* he or she leaves. This means that you will need a sales office on the premises or nearby with seasoned salespeople who understand that selling a fractional share is a different type of sale.

Once the prospective buyer is at your development, he or she needs to feel the magic immediately. Some developments have a special lounge for potential shareowners, setting the tone of "special treatment starts here." Scale models of the finished units add to their ability to imagine themselves there. The relaxed tour of the model unit and the development community itself must give your buyers a memorable taste test of what it would feel like to live there. You'll want to showcase the services and amenities. And if a buyer wants to talk to a shareowner in residence, you should make that happen. The sale of fractional properties is a low/no-pressure sale that, unlike timeshare sales, should be a positive experience. When potential buyers leave your property, each one should be rewarded with a take-home gift, such as a T-shirt, hat, or beach towel with your logo or brand proudly featured.

Once the sale is closed, the new owner should receive an elegant branded bag or take-home gift that holds the contracts, rules and regulation documents, and other sales materials, highlighting the development and the local environs. Completing the purchase should make the buyer so excited that he is anxious to tell his friends and family all about it—and these folks also may be interested in their own slice of paradise.

To that end, have a referral program in place. Word-of-mouth sales make up a large percentage of sales of fractional properties, so be sure to reward your buyers who share their great experiences with others. Share the wealth. Your buyers will want to tell their friends—let them know that they will be rewarded for it.

First impressions matter. In marketing your development, as well as in selling the units, you must make a positive impact beginning with the first face potential buyers meet through to the services and amenities you promise. And compensate your sales and service people. It will be reflected in the way they treat your guests.

MAKING YOUR DEVELOPMENT A PARADISE

The collection of people who will serve your shareowners includes everyone from people behind the check-in desk to the crew that cleans the pool—and it will take a team. You will be working with architects, construction teams, and experienced interior decorators. These are the behind-the-scenes team members who will ensure that your accommodations represent the height of luxury, from the furniture and appliances to the bath towels and bed linens.

Does One-Off Mean Double the Profits?

Inevitably I get asked the question, "What if I already own a second house or condo in Colorado that I don't use much. Could I profit by going fractional?" In the industry, this is called a *one-off fractional*, and I'd think long and hard before taking this route.

More owners mean more work! What once meant you needed to find one buyer for your full-ownership home, now you need to find four or six or eight or thirteen buyers. As I've said before, the buyer profile for fractionals is much different from that of full ownership, and fractionals are marketed much differently from "buy this house" or "rent this unit."

The time and money it takes to go through the legal and regulatory paperwork required to convert a primary residence into shared ownership is also considerable. Marketing and sales may be regulated by your state, so you need to know the law. You need usage plans that work for your location and comprehensive rules and regulations stating how the shares and common areas are to be used.

Fractional properties also sell at a premium, so high-end amenities with lots of services, provided and updated on an ongoing basis, must be in place. At a minimum, therefore, do your due diligence to find out what is required and allowed for you to fractionalize your wholly owned vacation home.

As the developer, you'll want to hire the best management company you can find—people who can oversee the day-to-day operations and treat *your* development like it is their very own. These team leaders will hire and manage the service providers who will make or break the quality of the shareowners' experience—the all-important concierge service, the housecleaning and restaurant staff, the groundskeepers, the spa professionals, and the local tours guides.

Your feasibility study and market research will indicate what types of special services and resort-living amenities are being offered by other fractional developments, resorts, timeshares, and hotels in the area. Making your property a paradise requires that your offerings meet and exceed that standard.

If your target shareowner travels with children, then providing a clubhouse for kids or teens is a wise consideration. If your buyer group is into health and fitness, then you need to offer membership to a top-notch health club, yoga studio, and full-service spa. If your development is a deep sea fishing destination, then make sure that you offer comfortable access to boats, fishing gear, people to clean the fish (and cook them), and a reliable, service-oriented crew. If it's golf or skiing, you need to provide the very best *experience* in customer service.

THE SKY'S THE LIMIT

The opportunities for new fractional development are exceptional. In fact, the market is developing so rapidly that it is hard for industry experts to keep up with the year-over-year changes. The success of *your* entrepreneurial endeavor depends on your careful analysis of your market, your buyers, your team, and your business. You need to know how to provide every one of your potential buyers with the chance to experience their very own slice of paradise.

While I am a fervent believer in following your instincts in life and in business, when it is time to put together a deal, I make the final decisions with my head after reviewing all the facts. Once an investment opportunity looks like a go, I call on my team of experts to review every aspect of my plan and confirm that the investment projections are realistic—and that they can be realized expeditiously and profitably.

I love being in the shared-ownership resort-home industry. From my first introduction to the world of fractional ownership, I have been motivated to help people realize the dream of owning their very own slice of paradise. If you share my motivation and you're ready to do your due diligence to develop a successful fractional property in the Pacific Northwest, the rain forest regions of Costa Rica, or the sunny coast of Mexico, there is a team of people waiting to work with you to realize *your* dream. Fractional ownership makes it all possible like never before—for you and for your shareowners.

CHAPTER 8

It's Time for Your Slice

Here's what I know with absolute certainty: Fractional ownership is revolutionizing how people choose to live their lives.

Americans used to look at retirement as some landmark at age sixty-five. After decades dedicated to the job, it was time to be put out to pasture, where leisure time was about collecting stamps, baking cookies, and maybe some traveling. A second home or vacation home might be a condo in some corner of a warm state or a cottage along a lake.

Today, that old model no longer fits with how we want to experience life. Baby boomers content in their W2 jobs realize that there's no value in postponing enjoyment of life until some arbitrary age and that their paychecks alone will not be sufficient to secure their financial future. Gone are the days when loyal employees had job security and the promise of a dependable pension, the standard during our fathers' working years.

My father could have been a brilliant entrepreneur, but he would never break away from the pack. He was an exceptionally talented self-made businessman. Most of his clients worked with him for twenty years or more, and like many workers of his generation, he was loyal to them. In my father's case, his strategy paid off, and he was able to succeed far beyond his own expectations.

As I look back on my father's life, I've thought about how he made regular business trips to Europe but never once stayed in a four-star hotel. Maybe it was his upbringing or being affected by the economic landscape of a very different twentieth-century America, but he always chose to play it safe. My first job out of college was as a programmer at IBM, and when I told him that I was going to work for "Big Blue," it was one of the proudest days of his life.

Unfortunately, my generation came of age being denied 5 percent raises while CEOs pocketed six- and even seven-figure bonuses. Downsizing, mergers, and competition from a global economy made "job security" a vague memory. Many of us have carefully reviewed the current corporate culture and decided to forge our own paths. I decided that I would rather be the one making the decisions about my financial future—and how I experience life—than risk following outdated trends and postponing second homeownership until age sixty-five.

When my employer downsized my position and I came

to Live Out Loud, I saw for the first time what it really means to be an entrepreneur and how you can be successful working for yourself. The work is harder at times, but it is also much more rewarding. In fact, becoming an entrepreneur is the single most rewarding choice I have made in my life.

Still, I bought my first "second home" while I was busy racking up the hours in a corporate job. Not long after my experience with Live Out Loud, I saw the raw potential for fractional development in Mexico and jumped at the chance to realize the dream of fractional ownership.

I love the *business* of fractional real estate, but what excites me most is that fractional ownership really has nothing to do with what we've known as "retirement." It's about how we want to experience life. No more waiting "until" or "as soon as." The time is now. Fractional homeownership is about realizing the dream—including one that means owning multiple homes in multiple locations. This is exactly what Andy and his wife Pat chose when they decided that it was time for their slice.

LIVING THE DREAM

An affluent Denver couple in their late fifties, Andy and Pat were both fortunate enough to retire early after decades in the media industry. If you asked them what their favorite pastime is, they would answer loudly and in unison, "Travel!"

While working in the corporate world, the couple purchased a timeshare in Aspen so that they could ski for a week each January. The arrangement worked well enough for them for awhile. Over time, though, it became increasingly difficult to match their available vacation time with the timeshare calendar, and dealing with the management company was anything but personal. It was stressful enough for Andy and Pat to coordinate their own busy work schedules, and when they were denied their desired timeslots two years in a row, they threw up their hands in frustration and sold their timeshare.

Now retired with more free time, the couple went online to weigh their options. They looked at vacation homes in Aspen, as well as in their other favorite spot on earth— Puerto Vallarta. While the properties they found on the Internet were beautiful, with the luxurious resort look and feel they wanted, they also decided that sole homeownership meant that they'd feel obligated to use the home they purchased. One thing they knew they wanted was to enjoy a *variety* of locations.

The next option they explored was destination clubs. They found a variety of companies with the deluxe resort locations they wanted, complete with almost palatial accommodations. They were willing to pay for what they wanted to experience, but the idea of sacrificing property ownership was obviously a waste of money. The idea of a destination club also felt a little cold, more like staying in a hotel than owning a personal oasis. A destination club might be high-end opulence at its best, but the concept didn't promise that welcoming, "at home" ambience they wanted.

The first time they explored fractional property online, they saw such terms as *shares* and *shared ownership* and clicked right off the website. It sounded way too much like a timeshare, and they'd been down that road before. One day, while Pat was having coffee with a friend, the topic of fractional real estate came up. To her surprise, Pat's friend had purchased a fractional condo in Vail, and she loved the property and all the services and amenities it had to offer— ski-in, ski-out access to the slopes, onsite spa and gourmet restaurant, daily maid service, and when she couldn't use her timeslot, a rental program run by the management company. When Pat heard how her friend *owned* her share and had already built equity in the year since buying it, she knew that fractional real estate deserved a closer look.

Today, Andy and Pat own multiple slices of paradise, and it was all made possible through fractional ownership. Every January they drive to their deluxe fractional chalet in Aspen to ski and savor their view of the Rocky Mountains. One month each year they travel to their luxurious seaside home just outside of Puerto Vallarta, where they snorkel, shop in the local markets, and take advantage of the "discover Mexico" excursions provided through their development. A weekend visit with friends in Napa last year resulted in their purchasing yet another plush condo in the heart of Wine Country. Now they can travel to California with other couples several long weekends a year to tour the vineyards or enjoy fine dining in San Francisco.

Andy and Pat chuckle when people ask them, "So, how's retirement life?" Andy often quips, "Life's never been better. We've put ourselves out to pasture in Aspen, Mexico, and California, and now we're thinking about looking at 'pastures' in Australia!" That's grazin' on the good life, and fractional ownership is all about the good life.

REALIZE THE DREAM

I am tremendously lucky that one of the first people I spoke with after I left my corporate job was Will Maddox, the business partner I introduced in Chapter 6 and my brilliant alumni coach at Live Out Loud. During our first conversation together, I told Will that my business goal was simply to replace my old salary, and he boldly told me that I was aiming too low. When I later told Will that I wanted to make $500,000 in my first year, which was double my old salary, Will once again told me to aim higher.

I said in exasperation, "Will, I can't possibly make a million dollars a year." And Will said to me, "You're right. If you tell yourself that you can't, then you can't."

Like every big, life-changing goal, it's what you believe could be real that makes realizing the dream possible. Will advised me to spend fifteen minutes every day telling myself that I could make a million dollars a year doing what I loved to do. I had to silence the inner and external "naysayers" and keep telling myself it was possible—even if I didn't have a clear idea of how I could make that income possible.

So I did what Will told me to do, and I came to believe. Not long after, I decided to focus on land development and discovered the magnificent properties that I'm currently developing in El Pescadero and Los Cerritos, Mexico. I made very close to a million dollars that first year, and my earnings have increased substantially since then.

Will has become an invaluable member of my real estate development team, my mentor, and my friend. When it was my turn to break away from the "pack" for the first time and launch my real estate career, his voice was the one consistently urging me to make the bold moves. It was Will who told me that I needed to block out any dissenting voices and ask myself what I really wanted. It was Will who believed in me before I believed in myself.

The most surprising thing to me about this whole process is how quickly your brain can accept a new reality if you are willing to make a big change in your life. Although I had to convince myself initially to dream big, I now accept without hesitation that I can lead a life that I couldn't even imagine just a few years ago. I am empowered by these changes and incredibly motivated to share my experiences with people like you—people who dream about owning a deluxe resort vacation home or who might be interested in embarking on a journey similar to my own.

You're ready. You're smart. And your dues are paid. The future is bright, and you *deserve* to embrace a new perspec-

tive on the picture of retirement and second homeownership. It's time to realize *your* dream.

As my friend Loral likes to say, "A year from now, you'll
wish you started today. Ready, GO!"

About the Author

Janet K. Fish, founder of Breakaway Enterprises, LLC, specializes in international land development and currently manages several fractional real estate projects in the United States and abroad. An expert in fractional real estate, Janet's primary passion is helping people realize their dream of luxury resort homeownership.

Janet is also a renowned instructor and master coach for Live Out Loud, a company that helps people achieve financial freedom.

To learn more, please visit *www.paradisebytheslicethebook.com*

www.ingramcontent.com/pod-product-compliance
Lightning Source LLC
Chambersburg PA
CBHW020207200326
41521CB00005BA/281